Cambridge IGCSE®
Literature in English

Russell Carey

Cambridge IGCSE
Literature in English

CAMBRIDGE
UNIVERSITY PRESS

CAMBRIDGE
UNIVERSITY PRESS

University Printing House, Cambridge CB2 8BS, United Kingdom

Cambridge University Press is part of the University of Cambridge.

It furthers the University's mission by disseminating knowledge in the pursuit of education, learning and research at the highest international levels of excellence.

www.cambridge.org
Information on this title: www.cambridge.org/9780521136105

© Cambridge University Press 2011

First published 2011
4th printing 2013

Printed in the United Kingdom by Latimer Trend

A catalogue record for this publication is available from the British Library

ISBN 978-0-521-13610-5 Paperback

® IGCSE is the registered trademark of University of Cambridge International Examinations

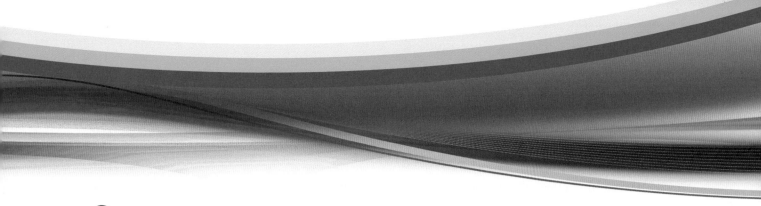

Contents

Part 1 Starting your Cambridge IGCSE Literature   **1**

Unit 1: How to get the most from this Coursebook   1
Unit 2: Cambridge IGCSE Literature: question types and
         assessment objectives   8

Part 2 Building your skills   **13**

Unit 3: Responding to Poetry   **13**
Reading for meaning   15
Exploring language and structure   27
Developing an informed personal response   43

Unit 4: Responding to Prose   **53**
Responding to characters   56
Responding to setting and mood   69
Responding to narrative viewpoint   76
Developing an informed personal response to a complete short story   85

Unit 5: Responding to Drama   **95**
Responding to characters and themes   98
Responding to structure and language   109
Developing an informed personal response   123

Unit 6: Developing effective writing skills   **128**
Critical writing   130
A closer look at essay technique   137
Writing empathic responses   142

Part 3 Preparing for assessment   **151**

Unit 7: Preparing for the Unseen Paper   **151**
Understanding and responding to Poetry texts   153
Understanding and responding to Prose texts   158
Working through a practice Unseen Paper   163

Unit 8: Preparing for the Set Texts Papers   **170**
Passage-based questions   171
General critical essays   176
Empathic questions   179
Be an active learner!   181
Developing effective revision strategies for your set texts   183

Unit 9: Preparing for the Coursework portfolio   **191**
What will you need to do for your Coursework portfolio?   192
Using your preparation time effectively   194
Writing your response   197

Glossary of key terms   **203**

Acknowledgments   **206**

Starting your Cambridge IGCSE Literature

UNIT 1 How to get the most from this Coursebook

Why study Literature?

Literature, like travel, broadens the mind, particularly when the writers you are studying come from countries around the world. The main criteria for selecting texts for Cambridge IGCSE Literature are that they should be well written (and therefore worth studying) and be written in English. One of the principal aims of the course is for you to enjoy the experience of reading and studying Literature.

How will this Coursebook help you?

This Coursebook is designed to be used in class or to be read as part of your individual private study. Its purpose is to help you develop the skills you need to succeed in your Cambridge IGCSE Literature course.

This book is intended mainly for students following the Cambridge IGCSE Literature (English) syllabus (0486). But much of it will still be relevant to you if you are following a Cambridge IGCSE Literature syllabus with a different syllabus code. You should check with your teacher which parts of this book are relevant to you.

Many of us find examinations among the most stressful experiences of our lives. This Coursebook aims to reduce the 'fear factor' associated with examinations. It will show you how careful preparation and effective revision can in fact increase your confidence and make the whole experience of examinations less stressful.

Key term

Texts, when used in this Coursebook, refers to a poem, a short story, a novel or a play. When studying English Language, you might work on different types of text, such as letters and newspaper articles.

The book is in three parts:

Part 1 ('Starting your Cambridge IGCSE Literature') introduces you to the study of Literature, to the Cambridge IGCSE Literature (English) syllabus, and explains how to get the most from using this Coursebook.

Part 2 ('Building your skills') helps you to develop the skills you will need for reading and responding to a variety of **texts**: poems, short stories, novels and plays.

This part of the book also gives you practice in developing your writing skills. It is important that you master these writing skills, as your understanding of the texts you study will be tested through your written responses.

Part 3 ('Preparing for assessment') takes a close look at the requirements of the various examination papers and of the coursework portfolio. This part of the Coursebook gives you specific guidance about how to write successful responses to questions, including advice about what examiners are looking for, and the criteria they use when awarding marks.

A **glossary** of key terms is provided for reference at the end of the book, and you should make good use of this.

Each of the Parts in the book is divided into Units. The content of each Unit is summarised below.

Unit 1: How to get the most from this Coursebook
This introductory Unit explains how the Coursebook will help you during your Literature course.

Unit 2: Cambridge IGCSE Literature: question types and assessment objectives
This Unit gives an introduction to the question types and assessment objectives used in the syllabus. You will find it helpful to familarise yourself with these assessment objectives, and to refer back to them as you progress through the course.

Unit 3: Responding to Poetry
This is the first main study Unit, and it is best for you to read and work through this Unit before the Units on Prose and Drama. One reason for this is that poems are generally much shorter than plays or novels, and even short stories. By studying the way in which poets write, you will be able to explore a complete text, and see how poets begin, develop and end their poems. This Unit will also introduce skills and learning strategies which you will go on to develop further in subsequent Units.

Whilst this Unit is not intended as an anthology, there is nonetheless a wide variety of poetry for you to read and explore. The Activities suggested and the questions asked are designed to develop your skills of analysis over the duration of the course. The more poetry you read, the more competent you will become at analysing poems closely. The poems chosen are the work of a variety of authors from different centuries and from different continents.

Unit 4: Responding to Prose

Except for one complete short story, the 'texts' for study in this Unit are extracts from longer prose works. They have been chosen to enable you to develop the skills you will need for reading and exploring the detail of longer prose works.

The Activities and questions in this Unit will focus on how writers begin their novels or stories, and how they establish the setting and mood, as well as how they develop characters and themes.

As with the Poetry Unit, the more you read, the more you will develop your skills of analysis. The questions will help you to develop appropriate vocabulary to use when analysing and writing about Prose texts, and methods for appreciating the ways in which writers present their material.

Your study of the complete short story in this Unit will help you to consider the ways in which writers not only begin and develop stories but also how they bring them to a conclusion.

The chosen prose extracts are by female and male authors, were written over the last two centuries and are from different parts of the world.

Unit 5: Responding to Drama

The extracts in this Unit are from plays by Shakespeare, written over four hundred years ago, and also from plays written during the last century, reflecting the kinds of plays to be found on the syllabus.

The Activities and questions in this Unit will help you to visualise the drama texts as plays that are intended for performance in the theatre. The extracts are designed to cover a range of key aspects that are important when studying drama texts: the ways in which dramatists begin their plays and establish settings and mood, as well as the ways they present characters and themes.

Unit 6: Developing effective writing skills

With this Unit, you will begin to consider in greater detail the specific requirements of the syllabus, starting with effective writing strategies. How successful you are in the examination will depend on how effective you are at communicating your ideas *in writing*. It is essential that you devote enough time over the duration of the course to developing your writing skills. Remember that it is your written responses that will be assessed in the examination and also in Coursework assignments (if you are following that particular option).

In this Unit you will look at the different sorts of questions you will find on set texts examination papers, and be given advice on how to tackle them.

Unit 7: Preparing for the Unseen Paper

This Unit builds on the skills you will have already practised in the previous Units on Poetry, Prose and Developing writing skills.

There are *two* questions on the Unseen Paper:

- one on a poem (or extract from a poem)
- the other on a prose extract.

If you are doing this option, you only have to answer *one* question, and the choice is yours.

You may find the idea of an Unseen paper rather daunting because you cannot revise for this paper as you can for a Set Texts paper. This Unit aims to reassure you by reminding you that you will have developed and practised the necessary skills for responding to Poetry and Prose in your work on the Poetry and Prose set texts.

In addition, this Unit will suggest useful strategies for how to prepare for the Unseen Paper, as well as giving you practice in answering examination-type questions.

Unit 8: Preparing for the Set Texts Papers

This Unit builds on what you will have learned in the previous Units, on responding to Poetry, Prose and Drama, and the development of your writing skills. It gives advice on how to revise your set texts effectively. Guidance is also provided on the different types of question that you will find in your Set Texts Papers, and how to prepare for these.

Unit 9: Preparing for the Coursework portfolio

The skills for reading Poetry, Prose and Drama texts have been developed in earlier Units, and these skills are all relevant for the texts you will study if you are doing the Coursework component.

This Unit provides clear guidance about the requirements for Coursework and suggests effective strategies for planning and producing successful Coursework assignments.

Link

If you are preparing for the Unseen examination paper, you will not be doing Coursework. Likewise, if you are doing the Coursework option, you will not be preparing for the Unseen Paper.

Active learning

This Coursebook covers all the requirements of your Cambridge IGCSE Literature course and the skills you need to achieve success. It is tempting to wish you 'Good luck', but in fact your success will depend more on the following:

*   Detailed and thorough revision of your set texts
*   Development and practice of key skills.

This Coursebook will help you to develop effective learning strategies and to develop and practise the skills necessary for your success in Cambridge IGCSE Literature. It will also encourage you to take responsibility for your own learning. The following are some of the ways in which you can do this:

1   Read texts – such as the drama and prose texts – before lessons, if you can.
2   Begin your revision of texts straight away. After lessons, find time when you can re-read closely the sections of texts you have covered in class.
3   Read with a dictionary available nearby. This can be in print or online. Meanings of words are not going to become clearer unless you use a dictionary.
4   Be an active reader and make notes – lots of them! Then add to your notes as you re-read them. You might find that a reading log or a computer 'scrapbook' is a very useful addition to your learning.
5   **Annotate** copies of poems or pages from longer texts. This can be very helpful indeed – particularly if you annotate key words to show how the writers achieve their effects. For this reason, it is helpful to have different coloured pens, or highlighter pens, to differentiate between various types of notes. A useful starting point is to use one colour for notes about content, and another colour for key words which illustrate a writer's choice of language.
6   Read up on set texts, using the internet or library for research. Study guides can be helpful early on in providing an overview of the plot or characters. Remember, however, that such guides should not be used as a substitute for your own informed personal response to texts.
7   Read texts aloud. This is likely to be done in lessons, and it is more easily done with poems and plays than long novels. However, there is no reason why you should not read aloud key extracts from the novels you are studying. If you have time, you could even record your reading of some of your poems or key extracts from drama and prose texts. This would certainly be an excellent way to revise.

Activities

The Activities and guidance found in this Coursebook will help you to become better readers of texts. Together, they will encourage you to reflect not only on the content of what you read but also on the important role of

Key term

Annotate means to make notes providing *brief* explanations or comments.

the writer. Exploring the deliberate choices writers make in their writing will help you to sharpen your skills of analysis. It will also increase your enjoyment of the texts you study.

Various approaches to Activities are encouraged, including working in pairs and small groups as well as individual study.

In addition, you will find examples of students' responses to questions, together with feedback from an examiner.

Quick recap

In several of the Units, you will find 'Quick recap' sections. These provide a quick reminder of important key points that have just been covered in the Unit. They allow you time to reflect on what you have just learned, and to look again at any points you are not clear about.

How to use the Coursebook features

You will find several different features on the pages of this Coursebook. These are there to help you as you progress through the book, and through your Literature course. They usually appear in the margins alongside the main text, and they often refer to something that is on the page.

Here is a list of the different features you will find as you use the book:

Key term

When a key term is used in the book for the first time, it is shown in **bold**, and defined nearby in a 'Key term' feature alongside the text. All key terms can also be found in the Glossary at the back of the book.

Link

These features refer you to other pages or Units in the Coursebook. You might, for example, be encouraged to go back and recap information or guidance provided earlier in the book, to remind yourself of what you learned in earlier Units. Ideas, terms and skills are often relevant to more than one Unit.

Tip

These features give you helpful advice and hints on studying, examinations and other aspects of your Literature course. These often build on the information given in the main text.

Extension

These features suggest useful learning Activities you could do on your own or perhaps working with another student. You are not required to do these activities, but they are there if you wish to have a go, and have the time to do them.

Further Reading

These features point you in the direction of other poems, plays and prose texts you may like to read for your own enjoyment or interest. You will be very busy during your IGCSE course, with other subjects as well as Literature, but you might find time to dip into some of the texts that are recommended. If you find something you like, you could return to reading it after you have finished your IGCSE course. Many students find that study of Literature at this level is just the beginning of a lifelong interest in reading.

UNIT 2 Cambridge IGCSE Literature: question types and assessment objectives

Objectives

In this unit, you will:

- become familiar with the different types of question in Cambridge IGCSE Literature

- consider carefully the course's assessment objectives.

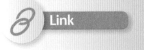

You will find specific advice about how to tackle the various types of question in the following Units:

Unit 7: Preparing for the Unseen Paper

Unit 8: Preparing for the Set Texts Papers

Unit 9: Preparing for the Coursework portfolio.

There are three different routes through the Cambridge IGCSE Literature syllabus. Your teacher will tell you which of the three routes you will be taking, and will provide you with more details about the requirements for each component. You can also refer to the current version of the syllabus on the web at www.cie.org.uk (under 'Cambridge IGCSE', and then 'English – Literature').

Whichever route you are taking, there is information in this Unit to help you.

What types of questions will you have to answer?

The types of questions you will be given in Cambridge IGCSE Literature are listed here. You will find further detailed guidance about how to answer each type of question in the later Units in this Coursebook.

Passage-based questions

You will find these questions for all set texts. Poetry questions will focus on a single poem, or occasionally an extract from a longer poem. Some Drama and Prose questions will ask you to focus exclusively on an extract from the text; other questions will expect you to analyse the passage in detail but also make some reference to how the passage fits into the overall text.

General essay questions

These are also provided for all set texts. Some Poetry questions ask you to focus on one poem whilst others will require you to comment on aspects of two poems. But where you are required to comment on two poems, you will not be expected to compare them.

Coursework tasks are very often similar to general essay questions.

Empathic questions

These are set only on Drama and Prose set texts, and never on Poetry texts. Empathic questions give you the opportunity to engage creatively with a text by writing as if you were one of the characters.

Empathic questions may be set for Coursework.

Unseen questions

Those of you taking the Unseen Paper will be taught how to answer Unseen questions. These are similar to the passage-based questions on set texts, and require skills of close analysis. The key difference is that you will have studied your set texts, whereas you will not have seen an unseen text before the exam.

Assessment objectives

All subjects have their own specific assessment objectives (AOs). These list the necessary skills that you must demonstrate in the examination and Coursework components. The assessment objectives for Cambridge IGCSE Literature are listed below, together with a detailed explanation of what they mean in practice.

Examination questions and coursework tasks are designed in such a way that they cover all of the assessment objectives.

Assessment objective (AO)	What it means for you
AO 1 Show detailed knowledge of the content of literary texts in the three main forms (Drama, Poetry and Prose)	You need to have a thorough grasp of the detail of the texts you study. You need to read your texts for the Set Text Paper(s) at least twice. The work you do throughout the course will help you to get to grips with the relevant detail, but you must be prepared to re-read your set texts carefully.
AO 2 Understand the meanings of literary texts and their contexts, and explore texts beyond surface meanings to show deeper awareness of ideas and attitudes	Your close reading of texts, together with written analysis, throughout the course will strengthen your appreciation of the themes and ideas.

Assessment objective (AO)	What it means for you
	You will need to go beyond the simple re-telling of the story, describing of characters or explaining the content of a poem.
	The skills covered in this book will help you to look for deeper meanings and to consider alternative interpretations.
	From your reading you will discover something about the context of the texts you read. You will only ever have to write about contexts that arise in the texts themselves.
AO 3 Recognise and appreciate ways in which writers use language, structure and form to create and shape meanings and effects	Most questions have an explicit focus on the techniques writers use to convey their subject-matter. In their plays, poems, short stories and novels, writers make careful choices about language and structure in order to achieve the particular effects they desire. The Units on Responding to Poetry, Prose and Drama will help you to appreciate how writers set out to produce certain responses in readers: perhaps, for example, to shock or amuse us.
	This assessment objective tests your powers of close reading and analysis. In answers to **passage-based, general essay** and **Unseen** questions you will need to make brief references to the text and comment precisely on the effects of the key words you quote.
	All questions, apart from empathic ones, make explicit mention of the writer. The writer is in charge, after all; the characters and ideas in texts do not exist independently of the writer.
	In **empathic questions,** your appreciation of the writer's craft can be assessed implicitly by how successful you are at conveying a recognisable voice for a particular character at a specific moment in the play or novel or short story.

Assessment objective (AO)	What it means for you
AO 4 Communicate a sensitive and informed personal response to literary texts	You are expected to give *your* genuine and considered response to the question you are asked, and to answer the question that has been asked rather than one you wish had been asked. This is not a subject where answers can be learned, or 'model' answers given. You certainly should not expect your teacher to provide you with ready-made views and opinions. An *informed* personal response means that you must provide detailed evidence from the text to support *your* views.

Developing your skills over the course

In studying Literature, you will discover that it is not easy to progress straight to Grade A. Your skills will develop, along with your confidence, over the duration of the course. This is an obvious point to make, but is easily forgotten by students if one of their first pieces of work is given a disappointing grade. It is perhaps easier to progress more quickly to the higher grades in subjects other than Literature.

If you work conscientiously in the ways that this Coursebook recommends, then you should acquire a detailed knowledge of your set texts. This book will help you to develop the skills necessary for tackling any type of question you will face.

We hope you will find much to enjoy in your study of Literature.

PART 2 Building your skills

UNIT 3 Responding to Poetry

Objectives

In this Unit, you will:

- read closely a range of poems
- develop the skills you need for responding sensitively to the meanings of poems
- analyse the ways poets use language and structure to create meanings
- use appropriate terminology when responding to Poetry
- gain confidence in giving informed personal responses to poems.

The following paragraphs will help you understand the objectives of this Unit in more detail, and explain how each section of the Unit will help you to develop the knowledge and skills you need when reading and responding to Poetry.

Read closely a range of poems

In this Unit you will work through a range of poems from different times and different places in the world. What these poems have in common is that they were all written in English. Most of the poems in this Unit are traditional poems; others are more recent poems.

You will need to provide detailed responses to Poetry in your Set Text, Paper 1 or Paper 4.

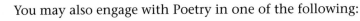

You may also engage with Poetry in one of the following:

- Set Text, Paper 5
- Unseen Paper
- Coursework component.

Respond sensitively to the meanings of poems

As you study the poems in this Unit, you will be introduced to the skills of close reading and **analysis**, which you need for success in this subject.

There are activities on each poem, which begin with the instruction to read the poem carefully. If you are reading the poem to yourself, get into the habit of sounding out the words in your head, emphasising each word. In addition, you should take the opportunity to read the poems aloud. Pay close attention not only to the sounds of words but also to the **rhythm** of lines and **stanzas**.

Analyse the ways poets use language and structure

The actual content of what you read is important, but in your writing about Poetry you will also be tested on your ability to analyse. This Unit will help you develop the skills you need for exploring the language and structure of poems.

You are encouraged to do similar activities to those in this Unit if you are studying Poetry for Coursework or as preparation for the Unseen examination paper. In this way, you can transfer the skills you develop in this Unit to other parts of your IGCSE Literature course. The main point to remember is that the writers are in charge of the material they write. Poets make deliberate choices about the words they use and the way they organise their poems. Writers may wish to amaze or shock you, to make you smile or to make you, the reader, respond in many different ways. They often intend to create different effects within the same poem.

You need to show that you can analyse the choices writers make and the effects they achieve in their writing. This Unit will encourage you to explore these effects very closely. Unit 6, 'Developing effective writing skills', will help you to organise your ideas when tackling the kind of extended written work which is required for both examination and Coursework.

Use appropriate terminology when responding to Poetry

This Unit will introduce you to terms that will be useful when discussing literature in general (e.g. metaphor, viewpoint) and to terms that will help you more specifically when exploring Poetry (e.g. stanza, sonnet). Remember that it is never enough just to say that a writer used personification or alliteration; more important is the reason *why* a writer uses these devices. You should also remember that you will receive no credit for using literary terms that do not actually contribute to your appreciation of Poetry.

These points will be explored more thoroughly later.

Gain confidence in giving informed personal responses to poems

The study of Literature rewards your ability to offer informed personal responses to the poems (and other texts) you read. An 'informed' response means that you must argue your point of view carefully. This requires you to support the points you make with brief but detailed references to the poems. You will not receive credit for simply repeating the views of your teacher or ideas found in the many available study guides, in print and online. *You* are responsible for arguing *your* own point of view, and for providing relevant evidence from the poems to support *your* argument.

This Unit will show you how to:

- ask the right questions when reading poems on your own
- analyse the effects poets create for their readers
- use evidence from the poems to support your own views.

The importance of active learning

You should make the effort to be an active learner. This means that you should be prepared to refer to the dictionary, whenever necessary, to look up unfamiliar words. In this Unit you will find that some poems have glossaries to explain difficult or archaic words. For other poems in the Unit, you will be responsible yourself for finding the meanings of unfamiliar words. An active learner will not simply read a text passively and ignore the detail. They will take active steps to explore the detail within the text. They will read with a pen or keyboard nearby, and note down their ideas.

The Activities in this Unit will help you to become familiar with the details of poems. For example, you will be asked to use lists, tables and mind maps, and to adopt a methodical approach to the way you annotate poems. These approaches will help you to understand both the surface and deeper meanings of the poems you read.

 Reading for meaning

Poetry is a good place to begin our close study of **texts** since the poems we will be looking at are all relatively short. They will therefore allow you to explore carefully the meanings of complete texts. In so doing, you will be able to consider how poets begin, develop and end their poems.

 Link

The skills of close reading and analysis will be developed further in Units 4 and 5: 'Responding to Prose' and 'Responding to Drama'.

 **Key term**

Archaic words are those which are no longer in use. Look out, too, for words which are still used, but where the meaning has changed. For example, the word 'awful' used to mean 'full of awe' (that is, inspiring wonder); nowadays we use it to mean that something is extremely bad.

Strategies are the approaches you use when studying texts effectively. This Coursebook will suggest strategies to help you as you study your Literature texts.

Some students find the poems they study in their early Literature lessons quite difficult. This is not something you should be concerned about; many past students have, at first, had a similar experience when reading Poetry. There are, however, ways to make the experience of reading Poetry less frightening. As you study the first three poems in this Unit, you will be introduced to various **strategies** that will help you to understand the meanings that poets set out to communicate.

The first reading of a poem is crucial. You must concentrate on reading the words on the page. Sometimes your teacher or a fellow student will provide the first reading; on other occasions, you will be asked to read a poem silently to yourself. Reading to yourself is the situation you would be faced with when sitting the Unseen Paper and choosing to attempt the Poetry question.

One of the skills you need to practise frequently throughout your course is reading texts closely. It helps if you read the words and sounds and lines of poems 'aloud' inside your head.

As you read Poetry, you need to focus on *two* important aspects:

- The content – what the poem is about
- The words and sounds the poet uses to create certain effects.

The following section of this Unit will help you to put into practice all of the guidance you have been given so far.

When reading Poetry, pause at the ends of lines only where there is punctuation, such as a comma or full stop. This is important whether you are reading silently or aloud. It would be a mistake to stop and pause at the end of each line of a poem. Such an approach would get in the way of understanding what the poet has to say.

Look at lines 2, 3 and 4 of the first poem, *Afternoons*. There would be no reason to pause at the end of the second or third lines, but a pause would make sense at the end of line 4, which is marked by a full stop.

How do you think this photograph reflects some of the ideas in Larkin's poem?

Tip

It is not a good idea to try to listen to music or watch television at the same time as reading and studying poems, or any literary texts. You should read without any distraction if you are to concentrate closely on what the poet has written. Switch off your phone!

AFTERNOONS
by Philip Larkin

Summer is fading:
The leaves fall in ones and twos
From trees bordering
The new recreation ground.
In the hollows of afternoons   5
Young mothers assemble
At swing and sandpit
Setting free their children.

Behind them, at intervals,
Stand husbands in skilled trades,   10
An estateful of washing,
And the albums, lettered
Our Wedding, lying
Near the television:
Before them, the wind   15
Is ruining their courting-places

That are still courting-places
(But the lovers are all in school),
And their children, so intent on
Finding more unripe acorns,   20
Expect to be taken home.
Their beauty has thickened.
Something is pushing them
To the side of their own lives.

Exploring AFTERNOONS by Philip Larkin

The purpose of the following Activities is to show you how to reach a fuller understanding of the poem.

The first Activity asks you to provide a general overview of the poem's content.

 Tip

Remember, the examination is not trying to catch you out; it is designed so that you can demonstrate your skills of analysis. In the Unseen Paper, difficult words are therefore explained for you in a glossary. You will find similar glossaries alongside poems and other texts in this Coursebook.

❶ Read the poem *Afternoons* carefully, and then read it again. Then answer the following questions. Remember that even very experienced readers might not fully understand a text the first time they read it.

How much of the poem do you think you understand? About half of it? Or more than half? Or less than half?

Write a summary of what you think the poem is about, in no more than two sentences.

2 During the first reading of a poem, it is important to note any unfamiliar or difficult words. You will see that once you have the correct meanings of these words, your overall understanding increases.

You may already be familiar with the meanings of the words used in a poem. In such cases, it is often still worth using a dictionary to look up the precise meaning that is relevant for the particular poem you are studying. This allows you to get as clear an understanding of the poem's meaning as possible.

▶ Consult a dictionary to find the relevant meanings for the following words. Write your answers concisely in a table like this one:

Words	Relevant meaning
recreation ground	a piece of public land where children play games
hollows	
assemble	
estateful of washing	housing estate full of washing
trades	
courting-places	
intent on	

Tip

All writers make deliberate choices about language and structure. This Unit on Poetry and the following two Units, on Prose and Drama, will give you opportunities to explore how writers use language and structure to create particular effects.

The Activities in this Unit will help you understand two key things about responding to Poetry:

* What to look for in a poem
* What to say about the poem.

Here are two important questions that are always relevant when exploring any poem:

* What does the poem have to say?
* How does the poet make deliberate choices about language and structure to create certain effects when communicating their ideas?

In your essays, you will need to tackle both these questions. In fact, you will need to spend more time on the second question, as will become clear later. In Activity 3 you will be considering the first of these questions; Activities 4–6 will help you to think about how to approach the second question.

3 Draw a mind map outlining the content for each of the three stanzas of *Afternoons*. Use a separate sheet for each stanza. Leave some space towards the edges of each sheet to make further notes for Activity 5.

Here is an example of a mind map for stanza 1:

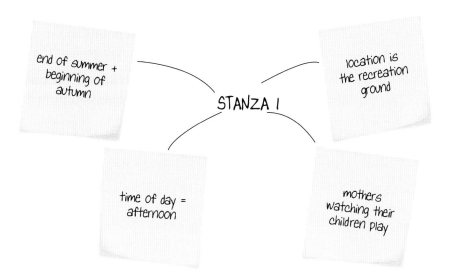

④ This Activity approaches the poem's content from a different angle.

Poems often present us with contrasts. In this poem, Larkin contrasts the lives of the parents with the lives of their children.

▶ List the points that Larkin makes about parents and children in a table like this one. Add to the points that are given below.

Parents	Children
Afternoons are empty for the mothers.	Afternoons are a time for play.
Mothers' lives are dictated by the needs of their children.	The children are 'set free' by their mothers.

⑤ The Activities so far have shown you ways you can read a poem closely so that it gradually reveals its meaning. Reading and writing go together. Active learners make notes about different aspects of the poem, and recognise that it takes more effort than one reading to give them a detailed understanding of the poem.

For this Activity, return to the mind map you created in Activity 3.

▶ Using a different colour, add to your mind map the key words Larkin uses, together with brief comments on the effects of these words.

The use of a different colour will help you to see the difference between two important aspects of studying Literature texts:

- Straightforward points about content: *what* the poem is about.
- Points about language: *how* the poets present their ideas.

The content points answer the question 'What?', whilst the language points answer the question 'How?'

Look at how the original mind map for stanza 1 of *Afternoons* might be extended.

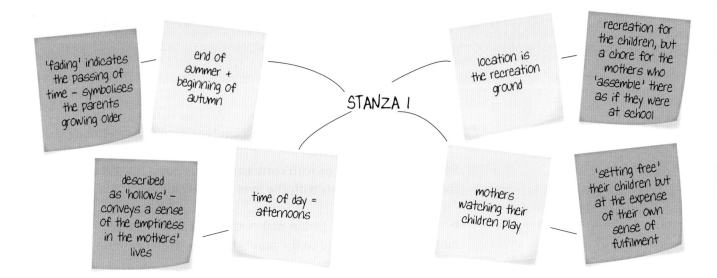

Tip

Activities like these help you to appreciate more fully the detail in the poems you are studying. Each time you re-read a poem, aim for an accurate reading out aloud. For your poetry set texts, you could record the poems being read aloud by you or by your friends and fellow students. These recordings would provide excellent revision.

6 The previous Activities have helped you, step by step, to go beyond surface meanings in the poem *Afternoons*. The final Activity on this poem encourages you to explore the poem's deeper meanings.

Write down concisely what you think the following add to the overall effect of the poem:

a the title
b the first line
c the poem's concluding lines:

> *Their beauty has thickened.*
> *Something is pushing them*
> *To the side of their own lives.*

PLENTY

by Isobel Dixon

When I was young and there were five of us,
all running riot to my mother's quiet despair,
our old enamel tub, age-stained and pocked
upon its griffin claws, was never full.

Such plenty was too dear in our expanse of drought   5
where dams leaked dry and windmills stalled.
Like Mommy's smile. Her lips stretched back
and anchored down, in anger at some fault –

of mine, I thought – not knowing then
it was a clasp to keep us all from chaos.   10
She saw it always, snapping locks and straps,
the spilling: sums and worries, shopping lists

for aspirin, porridge, petrol, bread.
Even the toilet paper counted,
and each month was weeks too long.   15
Her mouth a lid clamped hard on this.

We thought her mean. Skipped chores,
swiped biscuits – best of all
when she was out of earshot
stole another precious inch   20

up to our chests, such lovely sin,
lolling luxuriant in secret warmth
disgorged from fat brass taps,
our old compliant co-conspirators.

Now bubbles lap my chin. I am a sybarite.   25
The shower's a hot cascade
and water's plentiful, to excess, almost, here.
I leave the heating on.

And miss my scattered sisters,
all those bathroom squabbles and, at last,   30
my mother's smile, loosed from the bonds
of lean, dry times and our long childhood.

Exploring PLENTY by Isobel Dixon

Like *Afternoons*, this poem deals with the gap between generations: in this
case between a mother and her children. Here the speaker remembers how
she and her siblings used to run riot, to her mother's 'quiet despair'.

7 Read the poem *Plenty* carefully. Then match the words below to their appropriate meanings in the poem. Record your answers in a table like this one.

pocked   *clasp*   *compliant*   *stalled*
sybarite   *griffin*   *swiped*   *disgorged*

Word	Appropriate meaning
	stopped
	a mythical creature: a lion with an eagle's head and wings
	stole
	marked with blemishes caused by rust
	forced out from
	a person who enjoys luxury
	in agreement
	a clip which fastens

List any other words you find unfamiliar or difficult. Look them up in a dictionary, and write down the relevant meanings.

This is an essential stage in gaining a full understanding of the poem.

8 For each of the eight stanzas in the poem, write a sentence about what you learn from that stanza about the speaker's childhood. You could start with:

Stanza 1
The children were unruly, and the family had to be careful about how much water they used.

A summary of this kind will provide you with a concise overview of the poem's content.

9 How do the following lines help you to form an image of the mother? Write a comment on the effect of each of these lines.

a 'all running riot to my mother's quiet despair'
b 'Her lips stretched back / and anchored down, in anger …'
c 'She saw it always, snapping locks and straps, / the spilling …'
d 'Her mouth a lid clamped hard on this'

10 In class discussions and in your essays, you will be expected to support your judgements by referring to appropriate details in the poems you are studying. In Activity 9 you were given references to details in the poem that help you to form an image of the mother.

Key term

An **overview** is a general statement about the poem's content.

Tip

A solidus (or forward slash /) indicates the start of a new line.

Tip

Use quotation marks around the words and phrases you copy from the poem. This will make clear to the reader which is your own writing and which is the evidence you have quoted from the poem. For example:

The phrase 'stole another precious inch' shows how the children knew they were wrong in taking the scarce water.

Key term

A **turning-point** is a twist that signals a change in direction or a change in tone in a poem. These will often provide a useful starting-point for your close exploration of a poem's meaning and effects.

Link

There are poems later in this Unit with significant turning-points: for example, look at *Blackberry-Picking* (page 27) and *To His Coy Mistress* (page 43).

1 **antique** ancient
2 **trunkless** without the main part of the body
3 **visage** face
4 **pedestal** the base on which the statue was mounted

In this Activity, you have to provide the necessary textual evidence yourself to answer the following question:

▶ What impressions do you have of the children as you read the poem?

Support your answer to this question with reference to relevant words and phrases in the poem.

⑪ Re-read the final two stanzas of *Plenty*. The word 'Now' at the beginning of stanza 7 indicates a **turning-point** in the poem. There is a shift in time from the speaker's childhood to the present day.

Make a list of references from the poem showing how the author points out differences between the present day and her past. Start with:

- The bath is fuller now and she uses bubble bath.
- She regards herself as a self-indulgent person wallowing in luxury.

⑫ Write a brief paragraph in which you compare the speaker's attitude towards her mother at two different times:

a When the speaker was a child
b When the speaker is an adult.

⑬ Write about 200 words in response to the following question, remembering to quote from the poem to support your answer.

What do the words used by Dixon make you feel about the mother and about the speaker of the poem?

OZYMANDIAS
by Percy Bysshe Shelley

I met a traveller from an antique[1] land
Who said: Two vast and trunkless[2] legs of stone
Stand in the desert ... Near them, on the sand,
Half sunk, a shattered visage[3] lies, whose frown,
And wrinkled lip, and sneer of cold command,   5
Tell that its sculptor well those passions read
Which yet survive, stamped on these lifeless things,
The hand that mocked them, and the heart that fed:
And on the pedestal[4] these words appear:
'My name is Ozymandias, king of kings: 10
Look on my works, ye Mighty, and despair!'
Nothing beside remains. Round the decay
Of that colossal wreck, boundless and bare
The lone and level sands stretch far away.

How does this image add to your appreciation of Shelley's poem *Ozymandias*?

Exploring OZYMANDIAS by Percy Bysshe Shelley

Afternoons was a poem about life passing by: Larkin described how the parents' beauty had 'thickened'. Their lives were no longer their own, as they catered to the needs of their children. *Ozymandias* by Shelley deals with the temporary nature of human life, though from a different viewpoint and on a grander scale.

14 Read the poem *Ozymandias* carefully, referring to the words that have been explained for you. In older poems such as this, look for archaic words which we no longer use or which have changed their meaning. For example, 'antique' in the poem is used as an adjective meaning 'old'; in modern English the same word is more likely to be used as a noun meaning 'an object that is valuable because of its age'.

On a copy of the poem underline other words you find difficult and look them up in a dictionary. Annotate these words with the relevant meanings. For example:

artist who creates images by carving, e.g. in stone

Tell that its <u>sculptor</u> well those <u>passions</u> read

strong feelings

Tip

There are different places where you can look up the meanings of words:

- a dictionary in book form
- an online dictionary
- a mobile phone dictionary app.

By now, you should be used to having a good dictionary to hand as you study poems. For the remaining Activities in this Coursebook, it will be assumed that you know you need to look up unfamiliar words yourself.

15 Use the information in the poem to answer the following questions:

   a What parts of the statue are left standing?
   b Can all or only part of the statue's face be seen?
   c What does the description of the statue's face reveal about the character of Ozymandias?
   d Who is Ozymandias addressing in the words inscribed on the pedestal?
   e What do you think the inscription reveals about his character?

16 Much of the poem is highly visual – that is, we can picture clearly in our minds what is being described.

In order to be quite clear about the way Shelley has organised the material in the poem, put the following elements into the order in which they appear in the poem:

- The inscription on the pedestal
- The arrogant features depicted on the statue's face
- The remains of the statue looking tiny and isolated in the vast desert
- The expertise of the sculptor
- The description of the shattered statue.

17 Shelley provides a number of clues that give us an insight into Ozymandias' character. Create a table like the one shown below, and add your comments to say what the phrases listed reveal about his character.

Choice of words	Ozymandias' character
vast and trunkless legs of stone	
shattered visage, frown, wrinkled lip, sneer of cold command	
My name is Ozymandias, king of kings	
Look on my works, ye Mighty, and despair!	

18 Why do you think Shelley placed the short sentence 'Nothing beside remains' after a sentence which spans 9 lines?

19 It is helpful to look at two layers of meaning in any poem: surface meanings and deeper meanings.

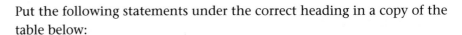

Put the following statements under the correct heading in a copy of the table below:

- A traveller recounts the tale of Ozymandias to the speaker.
- It is ironic that the sculptor's impressions of Ozymandias have survived rather than Ozymandias' impressions of himself.
- All that is left of the statue is the legs and pedestal.
- The statue stands isolated in the vast desert.
- Ozymandias was a power-crazed tyrannical figure who believed himself to be a god.

Surface meaning	Deeper meaning

Quick Recap
Reading for meaning

As you read a poem for your Set Text Paper or for your Coursework portfolio, follow the seven steps given in the table below. They will help you to uncover the surface and deeper meanings in the poem.

Step	What it means
1. Read the poem carefully	Sound out words in your head or by reading aloud. Avoid distractions. You cannot concentrate on the poet's words if you are also listening to music or watching television.
2. Look up unfamiliar words	Use a good dictionary – either print or online.
3. Annotate the poem	Make brief comments on the key words and ideas in the poem.
4. Write a summary OR Draw mind maps	Outline concisely what happens in each stanza or section of the poem. Think of the following: • What happens? • What is being described – a person, place, thing or event? • What are the feelings in the poem? • What are the ideas in the poem? • Who is the poem from and who is it addressed to?

5. Highlight clues about the poem's deeper meanings	Think of the following: • What are the poet's main feelings and ideas? • What is the poet's attitude towards the subject?
6. List the poem's deeper meanings	Create a bulleted list of the main feelings and ideas in the poem.
7. Read the poem	Aim for a polished reading. You will be able to do this since the previous steps have all helped you to arrive at a careful reading of the poem.

Exploring language and structure

BLACKBERRY-PICKING
by Seamus Heaney

Blackberries grow on thorny bushes.

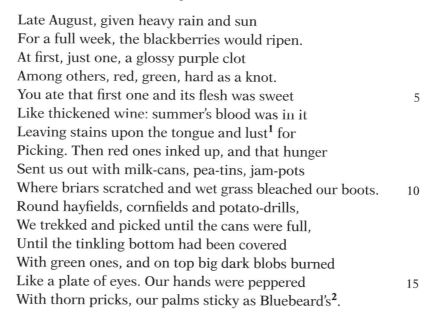

Late August, given heavy rain and sun
For a full week, the blackberries would ripen.
At first, just one, a glossy purple clot
Among others, red, green, hard as a knot.
You ate that first one and its flesh was sweet   5
Like thickened wine: summer's blood was in it
Leaving stains upon the tongue and lust[1] for
Picking. Then red ones inked up, and that hunger
Sent us out with milk-cans, pea-tins, jam-pots
Where briars scratched and wet grass bleached our boots.   10
Round hayfields, cornfields and potato-drills,
We trekked and picked until the cans were full,
Until the tinkling bottom had been covered
With green ones, and on top big dark blobs burned
Like a plate of eyes. Our hands were peppered   15
With thorn pricks, our palms sticky as Bluebeard's[2].

We hoarded the fresh berries in the byre.
But when the bath was filled we found a fur,
A rat-grey fungus, glutting on our cache.
The juice was stinking too. Once off the bush   20
The fruit fermented, the sweet flesh would turn sour.
I always felt like crying. It wasn't fair
That all the lovely canfuls smelt of rot.
Each year I hoped they'd keep, knew they would not.

1 **lust** strong desire
2 **Bluebeard** a notorious murderer and pirate-type figure

Tip

You need to show a detailed knowledge of the literary texts you study. Creating mind maps can help you to arrange visually the detail of the poem in a way that helps close study.

Exploring BLACKBERRY-PICKING by Seamus Heaney

The poem *Blackberry-Picking* describes a childhood pastime of collecting blackberries. It is written from the perspective of an adult looking back at his childhood.

20 Read the poem *Blackberry-Picking* carefully. The mind map below provides an overview of the content of stanza 1. Create a similar mind map for stanza 2.

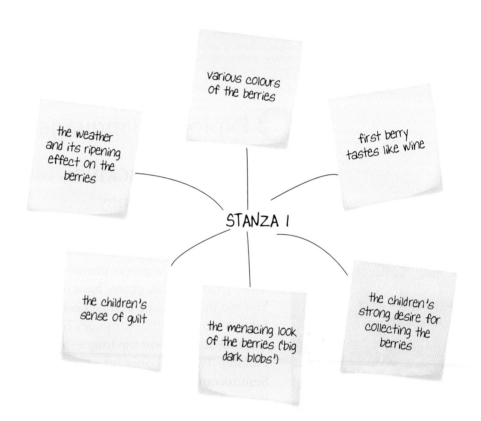

Key term

Imagery plays a central role in Poetry. On a straightforward level, you can picture in your head the literal images created by the words in the poem.

Other images poets use are not so literal, and writers use them to communicate their ideas more strikingly.

Poets deliberately choose the words they use, and it is part of your work as a student of literature to analyse carefully the effects created by those words.

In *Ozymandias*, Shelley uses **imagery** to create a number of meaningful images. As you read the poem, you can clearly picture the legs of the statue still standing, the face shattered and half sunk in the ground, the ruler's frown and sneer, and so on. In *Blackberry-Picking*, too, the poet helps you to see the vivid colours of the purple, red and green berries.

In *Blackberry-Picking,* Heaney uses non-literal images: similes, metaphors and personification. He does this to make the experience he describes more vivid to the reader.

A **simile** is the comparison of one thing to another. In this poem the flesh of the first berry is described in this way: 'its flesh was sweet / Like thickened wine'. The comparison with wine suggests the forbidden nature of eating the berries: perhaps this is something the children should not be doing. Your response to a poem involves looking closely at the choices of words made by poets, and considering their intended effects on the reader.

A **metaphor** is used to describe the first berry: 'a glossy purple clot'. A dictionary describes 'clot' as 'a thick mass of coagulated blood'. Heaney has deliberately used this word to create a rather disturbing effect. Remember that this is the first berry the child bites into!

Personification is used in the description of the 'big dark blobs' which 'burned / Like a plate of eyes'.

It is not enough simply to identify devices such as these; you must say why you think Heaney has used these particular words in the poem, and what effects he creates.

21 Examples of imagery in stanza 1 of *Blackberry-Picking* are listed below. In each case, say what type of imagery Heaney is using, and what effect he creates. Record your answers in a table like the one below.

Words	Type of imagery	Effect created
glossy purple clot		
its flesh was sweet / Like thickened wine		
summer's blood … Leaving stains upon the tongue		
red ones inked up	metaphor	This conveys the vivid saturated red colour of the berries, similar to red ink. The berries have the power to stain, in the same way as ink.
big dark blobs burned / Like a plate of eyes.	personification and simile	

Key Term

Alliteration - the repetition of consonant sounds in words which are close together.

Onomatopoeia - a word which sounds like the thing it describes.

Tip

As with imagery, you need to do more than merely spot and define sound devices such as alliteration and onomatopoeia. If you are to achieve high marks in essays, you need to explore:

• the effects such devices create
• how they help to convey the meaning.

22 As you read poems, you should be alert to the effects created by the sound of particular words as well as the rhythm of particular lines. There may be something significant about:

• the sounds of particular words and lines
• the length of words and lines.

Something unusual about the rhythm is always worthy of your attention. In such cases, the rhythm will clearly reinforce the meaning. Two common sound devices used by poets are **alliteration** and **onomatopoeia**.

▶ Read the following two lines aloud, and answer the questions which follow.

> We trekked and picked until the cans were full,
> Until the tinkling bottom had been covered …

a What sound is suggested by the use of alliteration: the repetition of the 'k' sound (indicated in red)? How does this help to convey the experience being described?
b Which word in these lines provides a good example of onomatopoeia, and why?
c How does the rhythm of these lines capture the experience being described?

23 The poem is written from the point of view of an adult who remembers his childhood pastime of collecting berries. From stanza 2 write down those words you think capture most closely the voice of the child.

24 How does the description in lines 18–21 show the boy's disappointment at what happens to the berries?

▶ Write down the key words or phrases, and explain the effect they have on you.

25 The excitement of picking the berries (in stanza 1) gives way to the boy's disappointment. He is upset at how quickly the excitement passed.

There are clues in stanza 1 that prepare the reader for the children's disappointment as described in stanza 2. Write a paragraph, outlining what these clues are. You might begin your answer like this:

The first clue is the description of a berry as a 'glossy purple clot' …

DAFFODILS
by William Wordsworth

I wandered lonely as a cloud
That floats on high o'er vales and hills,
When all at once I saw a crowd,
A host, of golden daffodils;
Beside the lake, beneath the trees,   5
Fluttering and dancing in the breeze.

Continuous as the stars that shine
And twinkle on the milky way,
They stretched in never-ending line
Along the margin of a bay: 10
Ten thousand saw I at a glance,
Tossing their heads in sprightly dance.

The waves beside them danced; but they
Out-did the sparkling waves in glee:
A poet could not but be gay,   15
In such a jocund company:
I gazed – and gazed – but little thought
What wealth the show to me had brought:

For oft, when on my couch I lie
In vacant or in pensive mood,   20
They flash upon that inward eye
Which is the bliss of solitude;
And then my heart with pleasure fills,
And dances with the daffodils.

What aspects of Wordsworth's
descriptions of daffodils can be seen in
this photograph?

Exploring DAFFODILS by William Wordsworth

Many poems deal with seasons of the year. *Blackberry-Picking* was set at the end of summer, in Ireland. This poem is set in England in springtime.

26 Read the poem *Daffodils* carefully to yourself, emphasising the sounds and rhymes as you do so.

27 Using a dictionary, match the following words to their correct meaning in the poem. Use a table like the one shown below for your answers.

sprightly   solitude   jocund   bliss   milky way   vacant   pensive

Word	Correct meaning
solitude	being alone
	faint band of light making up the night sky, made up of stars
	perfect happiness
	thoughtful
	lively
	empty
	cheerful

28 The poem begins with a description of the daffodils. It ends with the poet reflecting on what the experience of seeing the daffodils means to him.

   ▶ Pinpoint the precise moment in the poem where you think the description gives way to reflection. Explain why you chose that moment.

29 Explore the effects of these images in the poem. Then write up your own comments in a table like this one.

Image	Effect
I wandered lonely as a cloud / That floats on high o'er vales and hills	
a crowd, / A host, of golden daffodils	
Continuous as the stars that shine / And twinkle on the milky way	This simile gives the impression that the daffodils are so plentiful that they stretch as far as the eye can see. The words 'shine' and 'twinkle' show how bright and dazzling the daffodils appear to the poet.

Image	Effect
Tossing their heads in sprightly dance	
[the daffodils] Out-did the sparkling waves in glee	

Key term

Assonance is the repetition of *vowel* sounds in words which are placed close together. Remember that *alliteration* referred to the repetition of *consonant* sounds.

In your study of *Blackberry-Picking* you explored the effects of alliteration and onomatopoeia. Another sound device used by writers is **assonance**, which can be heard in the long 'o' sounds in the following line:

A host of golden daffodils

As you read this line, you can hear the repeated sound and it creates a sense of harmony. However, it is not so easy to establish a precise link between sound and meaning in this example. The best advice, therefore, is to focus on the meaning. There is no credit given in exams for making exaggerated or generalised claims about the sound devices poets use.

Tip

Effects created by sound will be easier to comment on in some examples than in others. In essays, it is sensible to focus on those examples where you have something useful to say about the way sound reinforces the meaning. Remember there is no credit given for simply listing sound devices (for example, that there is alliteration of the 'b' sound in the final two lines of stanza 1), without commenting on the effects these have.

30 Look at the following lines from *Daffodils*:

> *Beside the lake, beneath the trees,*
> *Fluttering and dancing in the breeze.*

Write down examples of the following in these lines:

- alliteration
- assonance
- onomatopoeia.

For each example, comment on the effects Wordsworth creates.

31 The poem *Daffodils* has a highly regular structure, with a regular **rhyme** scheme.

In each stanza the first and third lines rhyme at the end, as do the second and fourth. The final two lines (fifth and sixth) also rhyme, giving a sense of completion to each stanza. Note that 'glee' and 'company' in stanza 3 are not full rhymes unless you force the pronunciation of the second word. (Interestingly, in stanza 4 'mood' and the final syllable of 'solitude' are not full rhymes for UK speakers, but might be for US speakers of English.)

▶ Which pair of rhyming lines do you think is most effective, and which pair least effective? Give reasons for your answers.

Key term

Rhyme is the use of similar sounds for words or endings of words: for example 'trees' and 'breeze', and 'hills' and 'daffodils'.

Tip

Comment on the rhyme scheme only if you have something useful to say. The rhyming of 'trees' and 'breeze' in stanza 1 of *Daffodils*, for example, may well conjure up the sound made by the 'fluttering' leaves.

However, it is best to avoid generalisations such as: 'The stanza has an ABABCC rhyme scheme'. This sort of comment does not in itself really add to an appreciation of the poem.

32 In order to dig deeper into the meaning of the poem, explain why you think Wordsworth uses the following words:

wealth (in line 18)
pensive mood (in line 20)
that inward eye / Which is the bliss of solitude (in lines 21-22)

From Dorothy Wordsworth's diary, for 15 April 1802. Can you pick out any phrases that echo those in her brother William's poem *Daffodils*?

Further reading

This extract is from the diary entry made by William's sister, Dorothy Wordsworth, on 15 April 1802. Part of this extract (from '& at last …') can be seen in the original diary above.

*The wind was furious ... the Lake was rough ... When we were
in the woods beyond Gowbarrow park we saw a few daffodils
close to the water side, we fancied that the lake had floated
the seeds ashore & that the little colony had so sprung up –
But as we went along there were more & yet more & at last
under the boughs of the trees, we saw that there was a long
belt of them along the shore, about the breadth of a country
turnpike road. I never saw daffodils so beautiful they grew
among the mossy stones about & about them, some rested
their heads upon these stones as on a pillow for weariness &
the rest tossed & reeled & danced & seemed as if they verily
laughed with the wind that blew upon them over the Lake,
they looked so gay ever glancing ever changing.*

You can find more of Dorothy Wordsworth's diary on the internet.

 **Extension**

Romantic poets such as Wordsworth drew great inspiration from nature.
Fellow poet Samuel Taylor Coleridge adopts an almost devout tone in his
attitude towards nature in his poem *Frost at Midnight*. In this poem, Coleridge
imagines a world in which nature will be the best teacher for his young child.

Search for a copy of the poem in your school or local library and on the
internet. Then, using the close reading skills you have developed so far, read
the poem carefully. How do you think Coleridge portrays nature?

WHEN FORTY WINTERS SHALL BESIEGE THY BROW
by William Shakespeare

WHEN forty winters shall besiege thy brow,
And dig deep trenches in thy beauty's field,
Thy youth's proud livery so gazed on now
Will be a tottered[1] weed of small worth held:
Then, being asked where all thy beauty lies,   5
Where all the treasure of thy lusty days,
To say within thine own deep-sunken eyes
Were an[2] all-eating shame, and thriftless[3] praise.
How much more praise deserved thy beauty's use
If thou couldst answer 'This fair child of mine   10
Shall sum my count and make my old excuse,'
Proving his beauty by succession thine.
    This were to be new made when thou art old,
    And see thy blood warm when thou feel'st it cold.

1 **tottered** tattered, or old and worn

2 **Were an** Would be

3 **thriftless** worthless, or useless

Link

There are two types of sonnet: the 'Shakespearean' and the 'Petrarchan' (named after the ancient Roman poet Petrarch).

Look again at *Ozymandias* (on page 23) for an example of a Petrarchan sonnet.

There are two main sections to a Petrarchan sonnet:

1 the *octave* (of eight lines)
2 the *sestet* (six lines)

Re-read *Ozymandias* to see how Shelley has used the Petrarchan sonnet to organise his ideas. You will notice that the ninth line signals a shift in direction, or a turning-point.

Key term

The Shakespearean sonnet has 14 lines: three quatrains (each of four lines), ending with a rhyming couplet (two lines) which give a sense of completeness to the poem.

Tip

When reading any text for the first time, note your first impressions. Look at particular words or phrases and listen to particular sounds that you find striking.

Exploring WHEN FORTY WINTERS SHALL BESIEGE THY BROW by William Shakespeare

This **sonnet** by Shakespeare presents another perspective on the passage of time. You will notice that there is a clear sense in this sonnet of someone being addressed by the speaker of the poem.

Read the sonnet carefully. Two archaic words and one old-fashioned phrase are explained in the margin, but these are probably not the only words that you will find difficult, at least on a first reading.

> VVHen fortie Winters shall beseige thy brow,
> And digge deep trenches in thy beauties field,
> Thy youthes proud liuery so gaz'd on now,
> Wil be a totter'd weed of smal worth held:
> Then being askt, where all thy beautie lies,
> Where all the treasure of thy lusty daies;
> To say within thine owne deepe sunken eyes,
> Were an all-eating shame, and thriftlesse praise.

What do you notice about the spellings and the appearance of the letter 'S' in this early printed version of this sonnet?

The sonnet form shows how important structure is to poets and, therefore, to your analysis of the Poetry. Poets organise their thoughts by following the traditional structure of the sonnet. It is important to see how the poet uses the sonnet form to develop his ideas.

The following Activities will help you to organise a response to the language and structure of the poem.

33 On a copy of the poem, draw a line after each of the three **quatrains**: that is, after lines 4, 8 and 12. This will help you to see clearly the poem's structure. Write a summary of the content of:

- each quatrain
- the **rhyming couplet.**

34 Look at each quatrain of the sonnet in turn, and, on a copy of the poem, highlight the words and phrases you find striking. Annotate each of these by commenting on the effects each word or phrase creates.

For the first quatrain, your annotation might look like this:

'trenches' – metaphorically the wrinkles that cut into the face and take away its youthful beauty

'dig' makes it seem like a deliberate, destructive activity

'besiege' personifies a sustained battle against a human face, as if it is forced to surrender to the devastation caused by time

WHEN forty winters shall besiege thy brow,
And dig deep trenches in thy beauty's field,
Thy youth's proud livery so gazed on now
Will be a tottered weed of small worth held:

this continues the 'livery' metaphor in a shocking way; in time the livery will become old and worn, its pride vanished

the metaphor 'livery' conveys the idea that youth has a particular uniform which attracts admiring gazes; 'gazed' creates the impression of being looked at intently

35 Rhyming couplets give a sense of completion to a sonnet. How effective do you find lines 13–14 as a conclusion to the poem? Write your answer in no more than two sentences.

36 Rhyme can create a kind of musical effect as you read, and gives emphasis to the words which rhyme. Rhyme can also link words by their sounds to create certain effects.

▶ Write a paragraph in which you explore two rhymes from this sonnet that you find most effective, and explain your reasons for choosing them.

COME UP FROM THE FIELDS FATHER
by Walt Whitman

Come up from the fields father, here's a letter from our Pete,
And come to the front door mother, here's a letter from thy
    dear son.

Lo, 'tis autumn,
Lo, where the trees, deeper green, yellower and redder,
Cool and sweeten Ohio's villages with leaves fluttering in the
    moderate wind,   5

Where apples ripe in the orchards hang and grapes on the
    trellis'd vines,[1]
(Smell you the smell of the grapes on the vines?
Smell you the buckwheat[2] where the bees were lately buzzing?)
Above all, lo, the sky so calm, so transparent after the rain,
    and with wondrous clouds,
Below too, all calm, all vital and beautiful, and the farm
    prospers well.   10

1 **trellis'd vines** climbing plants held up by a wooden support

2 **buckwheat** plant producing starchy seeds

A portrait of a young soldier in the American Civil War.

3 **ominous** bringing bad news
4 **cavalry skirmish** a minor fight on horseback
5 **teeming** swarming, packed

Down in the fields all prospers well,
But now from the fields come father, come at the daughter's call,
And come to the entry mother, to the front door come right away.
Fast as she can she hurries, something ominous[3], her steps trembling,
She does not tarry to smooth her hair nor adjust her cap.   15

Open the envelope quickly,
O this is not our son's writing, yet his name is sign'd,
O a strange hand writes for our dear son, O stricken mother's soul!

All swims before her eyes, flashes with black, she catches the main words only,
Sentences broken, *gunshot wound in the breast, cavalry skirmish[4], taken to hospital,*   20
At present low, but will soon be better.

Ah now the single figure to me,
Amid all teeming[5] and wealthy Ohio with all its cities and farms,
Sickly white in the face and dull in the head, very faint,
By the jamb of a door leans.   25

Grieve not so, dear mother, (the just-grown daughter speaks through her sobs,
The little sisters huddle around speechless and dismay'd,)
See, dearest mother, the letter says Pete will soon be better.

Alas poor boy, he will never be better, (nor may-be needs to be better, that brave and simple soul,)
While they stand at home at the door he is dead already,
The only son is dead.   30

But the mother needs to be better,
She with thin form presently drest in black,
By day her meals untouch'd, then at night fitfully sleeping, often waking,
In the midnight waking, weeping, longing with one deep longing,
O that she might withdraw unnoticed, silent from life escape and withdraw,   35
To follow, to seek, to be with her dear dead son.

Exploring COME UP FROM THE FIELDS FATHER by Walt Whitman

Free verse has irregular lines and lacks a regular metre (such as the sonnet's iambic pentameter). In this poem, you can see at a glance that Whitman exercises total freedom in deciding how long his lines and stanzas will be. It is important to remember that free verse is used to reinforce the meaning.

In the poem by Shakespeare *When forty winters shall besiege thy brow*, the poet's ideas were developed using the traditional and regular form of the sonnet. The structure of this poem, by Walt Whitman, is very different. It is written in **free verse**. The poem captures the feelings of losing a family member in a war, in this case the American Civil War (1861–65).

37 Read the poem *Come up from the fields father* carefully. Sum up in eleven concise sentences (one for each stanza) the 'story' of the poem.

38 How does the way in which the poem is structured contribute to its dramatic impact? Use evidence from the poem to support your views.

39 The mood of the first three stanzas is calm. In stanza 4 the mother comes to the front door 'right away', and a sense of urgency is created.

▶ Re-read from stanza 6 to the end of the poem. How would you describe the changing mood? Refer to specific lines to support your answer.

40 In free verse, poets have considerable flexibility. Their lines can be as long or as short as they need them to be in order to convey their ideas.

▶ What effect you think is created by how long or how short the following lines from this poem are?

a *Above all, lo, the sky so calm, so transparent after the rain, and with wondrous clouds*
b *Open the envelope quickly*

41 Select one short line and one long line from the poem (though not the ones in Activity 40). Then comment on the effects created by:

a the length of the line
b its position in the overall poem.

42 In lines 4–11, what picture is depicted of the life on the farm? Look carefully at the words, and write two paragraphs in which you comment on:

a words which appeal to the senses
b words which use sound to create strong effects.

43 In lines 16–28, explore the ways in which Whitman conveys the death of the son and the sadness it brings. Write a paragraph, using brief quotations to support your views.

Remember to put quotation marks around the words and phrases you select from a poem, and keep your quotations brief. There is no point in copying out large chunks of the text. Quote only the words that help you to make your points clearly and precisely.

44 What does Whitman make you feel for the mother in the final stanza? Write a paragraph, in which you refer closely to his use of language and structure within this stanza.

Extension

Re-write the poem as a drama script. Give careful consideration to the sequence of events and also to the layout of the dialogue and stage directions. This could lead to acting out the scene in small groups.

This Activity will help you to focus on the different features to be found in Poetry and Drama. When poems deal with people and the words they speak, this kind of Activity can be useful in exploring the detail of poems as well as enjoying acting out the scene the poem depicts.

TELEPHONE CONVERSATION
by Wole Soyinka

The price seemed reasonable, location
Indifferent. The landlady swore she lived
Off premises. Nothing remained
But self-confession. 'Madam,' I warned,
'I hate a wasted journey – I am African.'   5
Silence. Silenced transmission of
Pressurized good-breeding. Voice, when it came,
Lipstick coated, long gold-rolled
Cigarette-holder pipped. Caught I was, foully.
'HOW DARK?' ... I had not misheard ... 'ARE YOU LIGHT   10
OR VERY DARK? Button B. Button A. Stench
Of rancid breath of public hide-and-speak.
Red booth[1]. Red pillar-box[2]. Red double-tiered
Omnibus squelching tar. It *was* real! Shamed
By ill-mannered silence, surrender   15
Pushed dumbfounded to beg simplification.
Considerate she was, varying the emphasis –
'ARE YOU DARK? OR VERY LIGHT?' Revelation came.
'You mean – like plain or milk chocolate?'
Her assent was clinical, crushing in its light   20
Impersonality. Rapidly, wave-length adjusted,
I chose. 'West African sepia[3]' – and as afterthought,
'Down in my passport.' Silence for spectroscopic
Flight of fancy, till truthfulness clanged her accent
Hard on the mouthpiece. 'WHAT'S THAT?' conceding   25
'DON'T KNOW WHAT THAT IS.' 'Like brunette[4].'

Telephone booths such as this can still be found in many places in Britain.

1 **red booth** old-fashioned English public telephone booth
2 **pillar box** post box
3 **sepia** light brown
4 **brunette** person with brown hair
5 **peroxide** a bleach which dyes hair blond
6 **raven black** shiny black like a raven

'THAT'S DARK, ISN'T IT?' 'Not altogether.
Facially, I am brunette, but, madam, you should see
The rest of me. Palm of my hand, soles of my feet
Are a peroxide[5] blond. Friction, caused –   30
Foolishly, madam – by sitting down, has turned
My bottom raven black[6] – One moment, madam! – sensing
Her receiver rearing on the thunderclap
About my ears – 'Madam,' I pleaded, 'wouldn't you rather
See for yourself?'   35

Exploring TELEPHONE CONVERSATION by Wole Soyinka

In other poems in this Unit we can talk about the 'speaker', where we can hear one voice. In this poem we hear a narrator's voice recounting the circumstances of a telephone conversation between him and a woman who rents out property. The poem explores the prejudice sometimes encountered by immigrants in England in the 1960s.

45 Read the poem *Telephone Conversation* carefully. Write down the dialogue from the poem in the form of a drama script. You should concentrate mainly on the words spoken by the man and woman. You could set lines out like this:

MAN   Madam, I hate a wasted journey – I am African.
           [Silence.]

WOMAN   How dark ....? Are you light or very dark?

In pairs, read through your drama script, making sure you bring to life the characters of both the man and woman. In your reading capture as clearly as you can an appropriate **tone** of voice for both the man and the woman. The tone for each character changes over the course of the conversation. Your reading should reflect this.

46 Annotate a copy of the poem to show how Soyinka portrays the unpleasant character of the woman. Refer to:

a the words she speaks, and her tone of voice
b the words used by the narrator to describe her.

47 **Enjambment** is used several times in the poem. Explain what effects are created by its use in:

a line 11
b line 14.

Key term

Tone is conveyed in a poem by the poet's deliberate choice of words. Think of the tone of voice in which a particular word or line might be spoken. The tone can, of course, change during a poem. In your essays you should be able to discuss where, and why, such changes in tone occur.

Enjambment occurs where lines run on without punctuation and without a break in the meaning.

Tip

Examiners read a lot of Poetry essays where comments on enjambment say little more than 'The enjambment makes the lines flow'. This may be true, but more precise comments are required about what makes particular examples of enjambment so effective.

Link

Enjambment at the end of stanzas is generally more significant than elsewhere in a poem. Look at stanzas 1 and 4 in Ted Hughes' poem *Wind* (on page 49) for a good example of how enjambment enhances the content of the poem.

 48 In what ways does Soyinka use punctuation to powerful effect in the following lines?

1 *'HOW DARK?' … I had not misheard … ' ARE YOU LIGHT*
2 *Red booth. Red pillar box. Red double-tiered/*
   Omnibus squelching tar. It was real!
3 *'ARE YOU DARK? OR VERY LIGHT?' Revelation came.*

49 How effective do you find the structure of the poem in reinforcing its content?

Your responses to Activities 45–48 will help you answer this question.

Quick Recap

Exploring language and structure

When exploring language and structure as you study a poem, you will need to consider the six key areas listed below. It is not possible to impose an order for you to follow, as readers respond to poems in different ways.

You could use the following strategies to identify and comment on the these key aspects of language and structure in the poems you are studying:

- annotation
- mind map
- lists.

Areas to consider	Comment on the effects of …
Words appealing to senses	words appealing to sight, hearing, touch, taste, smell
Imagery	similes metaphors personification
Sound	alliteration assonance onomatopoeia rhyme rhythm

Mood	the atmosphere of the poem (e. g. joyful, sad, menacing)
	the tone of any 'voice' or 'voices' in the poem
	changes in mood
	changes in tone
Structure	organisation of content in stanzas / stages of the poem
	use of traditional (e.g. sonnet) or other forms (e.g. free verse)
	effectiveness of opening
	effectiveness of ending

Developing an informed personal responses

TO HIS COY MISTRESS
by Andrew Marvell

Had we but world enough, and time,
This coyness[1], Lady, were no crime.
We would sit down, and think which way
To walk, and pass our long love's day.
Thou by the Indian Ganges'[2] side.   5
Shouldst rubies find: I by the tide
Of Humber[3] would complain. I would
Love you ten years before the flood:
And you should, if you please, refuse
Till the conversion of the Jews[4].   10
My vegetable[5] love should grow
Vaster then empires, and more slow.
An hundred years should go to praise
Thine eyes, and on thy forehead gaze.
Two hundred to adore each breast: 15
But thirty thousand to the rest.
An age at least to every part,
And the last age should show your heart:
For, Lady, you deserve this state;
Nor would I love at lower rate.   20
    But at my back I always hear
Time's wingèd chariot hurrying near:
And yonder all before us lie

1 **coyness** reluctance to do what the man wants

2 **Ganges** river in northern India and Bangladesh

3 **Humber** an estuary in northeastern England

4 **Till the conversion of the Jews** i.e. forever

5 **vegetable** able to grow

6 **vault** chamber used for burials

Deserts of vast eternity.
Thy beauty shall no more be found;   25
Nor, in thy marble vault[6], shall sound
My echoing song: then worms shall try
That long-preserved virginity:
And your quaint honour turn to dust;
And into ashes all my lust.   30
The grave's a fine and private place,
But none, I think, do there embrace.
   Now, therefore, while the youthful hue
Sits on thy skin like morning dew,

7 **transpires** leaks out

And while thy willing soul transpires[7]   35
At every pore with instant fires,
Now let us sport us while we may;
And now, like amorous birds of prey,
Rather at once our time devour,

8 **slow-chapped** slowly eating

Than languish in his slow-chapped[8] power.   40
Let us roll all our strength, and all
Our sweetness, up into one ball:
And tear our pleasures with rough strife,
Thorough the iron gates of life.
Thus, though we cannot make our sun   45
Stand still, yet we will make him run.

Exploring TO HIS COY MISTRESS by Andrew Marvell

It is important when reading Poetry to consider closely your first impressions and think carefully about *why* you feel as you do. Looking up relevant meanings of words leads to a more accurate reading of the poem. This will help you to make *informed* personal judgements about the text.

Exploring the language of poems helps you to identify how writers create and shape meanings. This detailed analysis will help strengthen your response since you are focusing clearly on why the poet has chosen particular words, images and sounds.

These are skills that you have practised in the earlier sections of this Unit. In the remaining Activities these skills will be reinforced as you build your confidence in giving your own informed personal responses to poems.

50 In the poem *To His Coy Mistress*, published in 1681, a man addresses his lover, or 'mistress'. A key theme of the poem is that of time passing quickly.

Read this poem carefully, and write down the impressions you have of the speaker. Use evidence from the poem to support your views.

51 The poem is presented as unbroken text. However, you can see that there are *three* separate stages to the argument the man presents.

Copy the following table and in the right-hand column, summarise what the man is saying in each of the three sections of the poem.

Section	Begins with …	Summary of what the man is saying
1	*Had we but world enough, and time*	
2	*But at my back I always hear*	
3	*Now, therefore, while the youthful hue*	

Key Term

Hyperbole is the use of exaggeration for a deliberate effect.

Tip

Remember that 'images' means both the pictures the poet's words create in your mind, and also non-literal images – similes, metaphors and personification.

52 Annotate a copy of the poem, with concise answers to the following questions.

Section 1 (lines 1–20):

a What evidence is there to suggest that the man is being light-hearted?
b Comment on examples of **hyperbole**.

Section 2 (lines 21–32):

c How does the speaker's tone of voice differ from that used in the first section?
d What effects are created by the images here?

Section 3 (lines 33–46):

e Highlight and comment on the words or phrases which best sum up the man's attitude here.

53 As you read the poem, how does your impression of the speaker change?

Select evidence from the poem which supports each of the judgements below. Remember to explain how the poet achieves this.

a A light-hearted man dazzling us with his wit
b An arrogant, thoroughly patronising sexist.

54 There are a number of different dictionary definitions for the word 'quaint' in line 29. These include:

- 'charmingly old-fashioned'
- 'cunning'

- 'ingenious'
- 'pretending to be fussy'.

Discuss with a partner how these different meanings affect your reading of the poem. Which of these meanings comes closest to your impression of the woman who is being addressed in the poem?

55 Using the information collected in answering Activities 50–54, write an essay plan for the following question:

In what ways does Marvell memorably convey the speaker's thoughts and feelings in To His Coy Mistress?

De-constructing the question

It is essential that you consider the key words of any IGCSE question before you attempt to answer it. You must pay close attention to these key words as you answer the question.

Key words in question	Meaning
In what ways	You need to explore the ways in which Marvell uses language and structure to capture the speaker's voice.
memorably	This word reinforces the need to look at the detail of the poem and what is memorable about it.
Marvell	The author's name in the question reminds us that the poet is responsible for choosing the words. So an essential part of any essay is to focus on this particular poet's craft: how he uses words, images, sounds and structure.
convey the speaker's thoughts and feelings	An important focus is on the way the poet 'conveys the speaker's thoughts and feelings'. You will of course need to give your impressions of the speaker's voice and tone, and how it changes over the course of the poem. Look carefully at both the language and structure of the poem.

56 The following are examples from students' writing about the second section of the poem *To His Coy Mistress*.

Which *three* examples provide clear analysis – points which are both supported by reference to the poem?

1 In the second stage of his argument, the speaker conveys how quickly time passes in the dramatic metaphor 'Time's wingèd chariot', and this marks a significant turning-point in his argument.

2 Marvell uses similes, metaphors, alliteration and rhyme to draw the reader in.

3 The bleakness and emptiness of what he says comes after death is clear from the metaphor 'deserts of vast eternity'. The tone of voice is much more urgent in these lines; it is serious here, where it had been playful in the first section of the poem. The stark images in this section suggest that the narrator is trying to manipulate his mistress into doing what he wants.

4 He uses a metaphor:
'Time's wingèd chariot hurrying near'.

5 The speaker uses an unpleasantly patronising, even sarcastic, tone in the final line of the second section:
   'But none, I think, do there embrace.'
There is a note of derision that shows his real attitude towards his mistress. She would probably be better off without him.

The comments below show how an examiner responded to the students' writing. Clear analysis is provided in examples 1, 3 and 5.

1 This response shows a clear understanding; it offers clear analysis of the words and structure of the poem. It recognises the 'significant turning-point' at the start of the second section.

2 What the student writes is no doubt true, but the comment is far too general to be rewarded. There needs to be specific examples and precise comment on the effects of these.

3 This extended response is very perceptive. Comment on the bleakness of the 'deserts' metaphor leads to a comment about the speaker's tone of voice and his purpose in manipulating his mistress 'into doing what he wants'. A contrast between the first and second sections of the poem is noted.

4 The metaphor has been spotted and noted, but unfortunately this does not lead to analysis of the words and their effects. This is straightforward description rather than analysis.

Link

You can read more writing by students and comments by examiners in Unit 6: 'Developing effective writing skills'.

5 This student offers a strong independent
judgement based on her clear and well-developed
assessment of language and structure, as she
focuses on the tone of a key line in the poem,
at the end of the second section.

Extension

The speaker's message in the poem is to make the most of the present time
and not give too much thought to the future. A Latin phrase *carpe diem*
(meaning 'seize the day') sums up this theme. Using the internet or your
school or local library for research, see how this theme is also explored in
Robert Herrick's poem *To the Virgins, To Make Much of Time*.

ROW
by Carol Ann Duffy

But when we rowed,
the room swayed and sank down on its knees,
the air hurt and purpled like a bruise,
the sun banged the gate in the sky and fled.

But when we rowed,   5
the trees wept and threw away their leaves,
the day ripped the hours from our lives,
the sheets and pillows shredded themselves on the bed.

But when we rowed,
our mouths knew no kiss, no kiss, no kiss,   10
our hearts were jagged stones in our fists,
the garden sprouted bones, grown from the dead.

But when we rowed,
your face blanked like a page erased of words,
my hands squeezed themselves, burned like verbs,   15
love turned, and ran, and cowered in our heads.

Exploring ROW by Carol Ann Duffy

This poem takes a close look at what it feels like to row or quarrel. The
Activities below are designed to help you respond fully to the content,
language and structure of the poem.

57 Read the poem carefully.

Then list particularly striking words or phrases in a table like the one at
the top of the next page, and comment on their effects.

Word or phrase	Effect

58 On a copy of the poem use different colours to highlight examples of the following devices used:

- repetition
- onomatopoeia
- simile
- personification
- hyperbole.

59 Write about 300 words in answer to the following question. Use your responses to Activities 57 and 58 as a starting-point.

In what ways does the poet vividly convey the experience of quarrelling?

WIND
by Ted Hughes

This house has been far out at sea all night,
The woods crashing through darkness, the booming hills,
Winds stampeding the fields under the window
Floundering black astride and blinding wet

Till day rose; then under an orange sky   5
The hills had new places, and wind wielded
Blade-light, luminous black and emerald,
Flexing like the lens of a mad eye.

At noon I scaled along the house-side as far as
The coal-house door. I dared once to look up –   10
Through the brunt wind that dented the balls of my eyes
The tent of the hills drummed and strained its guyrope*,

The fields quivering, the skyline a grimace,
At any second to bang and vanish with a flap:
The wind flung a magpie away and a black–   15
Back gull bent like an iron bar slowly. The house

Rang like some fine green goblet in the note
That any second would shatter it. Now deep
In chairs, in front of the great fire, we grip
Our hearts and cannot entertain book, thought,   20

Or each other. We watch the fire blazing,
And feel the roots of the house move, but sit on,
Seeing the window tremble to come in,
Hearing the stones cry out under the horizons.

The phrase 'In what ways?' is sometimes used to begin literature questions. It is a different way of saying 'How?'. When considering the 'ways' writers 'convey' their ideas, you should consider the way they use language and structure.

* **guyrope** rope used to secure a tent to the ground

49

The poem *Wind* was originally published in the book *Remains of Elmet* (1979), which contained poems by Ted Hughes and photographs by Fay Godwin. How far do you think this photograph complements the poetry?

Exploring WIND by Ted Hughes

In *Daffodils* by Wordsworth, nature is portrayed in all its beauty and splendour. The poem *Wind* by Ted Hughes regards nature in a very different way.

For this, the final poem, you will use a number of strategies covered earlier in this Unit. You will need a copy of the poem *Wind*, and several pens of different colours.

The Activities in this Unit have stressed the importance of having a keen eye and ear for detail. It is this attention to detail which helps to reinforce the quality of your argument. There are only two Activities for this poem: an annotation exercise; followed by an extended written response to the poem.

60 Spend 20 minutes on this Activity.

Read the poem carefully, and annotate the following:

- The words which refer to time, starting with 'at night' (line 1)
- Sounds used to describe the wind
- Imagery used to describe the wind
- Descriptions of the people
- Effects created by enjambment
- Dramatic use of monosyllables.

Tip

For examination and Coursework questions, you cannot write everything you know or could say. There is a limit to how much you can write within the time allowed for the examination or the word count permitted for Coursework assignments. Learn to be selective. Choose the best material which answers the question most effectively.

61 Spend 50 minutes on this Activity.

Attempt the following IGCSE-type question:

How does Hughes powerfully convey the menacing nature of the wind in this poem?

Remember the following points as you write your answer to the question:

- Decide which material in Activity 60 you could use for this essay.
- Select the best material. You cannot be exhaustive in the time available and write everything that there is to be said.
- Decide on the best order in which to present your material.
- Write your response.
- Leave some time for checking through what you have written.

Quick recap
Developing an informed personal response

Different readers respond in different ways to Poetry. Examiners want to read what you have to say about *your* response to the poems you have studied. A disciplined approach to study helps you to develop a convincing and independent personal response – 'independent' because you offer your own judgements and you provide the support to back them up.

This flowchart shows the progress of a student's independent personal response. It starts with your initial reading and ends with writing a detailed analysis of the poem.

Read the poem

Record your initial impressions

Strengthen your reading by referring to a dictionary

Write a concise overview of the poem's content

Explore the effects of the poet's choices of language and structure

Write a detailed analysis of the poem

Further reading

Use your school or local library or the internet to read and research other poems by the writers in this Unit. You can find poems online by Shelley, Wordsworth, Shakespeare, Whitman and Marvell. You can also use the internet to find poems by modern poets such as Seamus Heaney, Wole Soyinka, Ted Hughes and Carol Ann Duffy.

Extension

Listen to poets reading their own poems on websites such as The Poetry Archive – http://www.poetryarchive.org

Unit summary

In this Unit you have learned how to explore both the surface and deeper meanings of a range of poems.

You have practised a number of strategies to help you to arrive at a clear overview of poems. These include looking up meanings; writing summaries and lists; annotating poems and creating mind maps.

Poets make deliberate choices in the words, images and sounds they use, and they think carefully about the way in which they structure their poems. In this Unit you have learned how to comment on the effects of writers' choices and not simply list the devices they use. You should also be able to use with confidence a number of terms that are helpful when discussing Poetry.

Finally, you have learned how important it is to give your own considered opinions. In studying Literature you are expected to do more than simply regurgitate ideas from your teacher or from study guides. So long as your opinions are supported by relevant evidence from the poem, examiners will enjoy reading your independent responses.

The next unit will build on the skills you have developed so far.

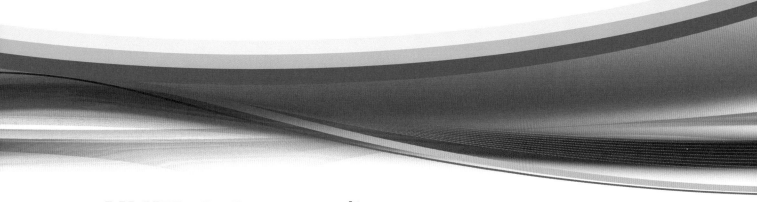

UNIT 4 Responding to Prose

Objectives

In this Unit, you will:

- read closely a number of extracts from novels and short stories

- develop skills you need for responding sensitively to Prose fiction

- analyse the ways Prose writers use form, structure and language to create and shape meanings

- use appropriate terminology when responding to Prose texts

- gain confidence in giving informed personal responses to Prose texts.

The following paragraphs will help you understand the objectives of this Unit in more detail, and explain how each section of the Unit will develop the knowledge and skills you will need when reading and responding to Prose.

Read closely a number of extracts from novels and short stories

In this Unit you will work through a series of Activities based on extracts from Prose texts by writers from different parts of the world. The extracts are from texts written in the nineteenth century right up to the present day. There is also one complete short story.

You will need to provide detailed responses to Prose texts in your Set Texts Paper 1 or 4.

You may also have to engage with Prose texts in one of the following:

- Set Texts Paper (Paper 5)
- Unseen Paper (Paper 3)
- Coursework Component.

Respond sensitively to Prose fiction

As you study closely the Prose texts in this Unit, you will develop further the reading skills and active learning skills introduced in the previous Unit on Poetry.

Some unusual or difficult words will be explained for you. For the meaning of other words you will need to refer to a dictionary. Remember this is an essential stage in developing a detailed understanding of literary texts. If you do not look up the meanings of unfamiliar words, your understanding will be incomplete.

Practise reading the extracts aloud in order to get the pronunciation of words correct. Think about what the words mean. Are they, for example, sad, joyful, angry or frightening? As you read, try to match the tone of your voice to the meanings of the words. Aim to capture a suitable voice for the words spoken by different characters. This is a useful stage for active learning, as it allows you to enter the minds of the characters.

Remember, too, that active learners write as well as read. Be prepared to use the note-making strategies introduced in Unit 3, 'Responding to Poetry'. The following strategies will help you to acquire a detailed understanding of the texts you study:

- Annotating copies of the extracts
- Making lists
- Recording information in tables
- Producing mind maps.

Link

Unit 6, 'Developing effective writing skills' will help you to understand how your ideas can be organised in written work for both the examination and Coursework components.

Analyse the ways Prose writers use form, structure and language

In the previous Unit, you considered *how* poets write as well as *what* they write. You explored the writer's craft – that is, the ways in which a writer uses form, structure and language to convey meanings. In Prose texts, too, it is important to consider the *ways* in which writers write as well as what they write.

In this Unit you will develop further the necessary skills of analysis. Some of the key areas you will consider are the ways in which Prose writers:

Key term

Some of the terms used in this Unit were introduced and explained in Unit 3 'Responding to Poetry'. You can also find them explained in the Glossary at the end of this Coursebook.

Other terms introduced in Unit 3 will also be useful when discussing Prose texts. For example:

Imagery: simile, metaphor, personification

Sound: alliteration, assonance, onomatopoeia

- begin novels and short stories
- develop plots
- present characters
- explore themes
- create settings
- convey mood
- sequence events
- use narrative viewpoint to tell their story.

These are important aspects to consider when analysing Prose texts. This is true whether you are studying examination texts, Coursework texts or unseen extracts.

You need to show that you can evaluate the deliberate choices Prose writers make and the effects they create. As with Poetry, the writers are in control of the words they use and also how they organise their content.

Use appropriate terminology when responding to Prose texts

In this Unit you will be introduced to a number of terms which are useful when discussing Prose fiction.

However, as with Poetry, it is never enough simply to identify the devices Prose writers use. Analysis means that you must consider the effects of the words chosen by the writers. This is more important than using the actual terms themselves.

Gain confidence in giving informed personal responses to Prose texts

Remember: 'informed' means that you must argue your point of view carefully. You need to support the points you make with the use of detailed, and preferably brief, references to the texts. It is your personal engagement with texts that is important. Do not only consider the views in study guides or those of your teacher, but develop your own ideas.

In the Set Texts Papers, you have to answer one of *three* questions which are set on each Prose text:

- The first asks you to explore in detail a passage from the text.
- The second question asks for a more general **critical response**. You have to support your argument by means of references to the text and analytical comment on the writing.
- The third question asks for an **empathic response**. Here you are asked to write as a particular character at a key moment in the text. You are asked to use a suitable 'voice' for your character, which means that what they say reflects the character's typical vocabulary, ways of speaking, and attitudes, and perhaps something of the era in which they live.

This Unit will show you how to:

- ask the right questions when reading Prose fiction
- analyse the language and structure used by novelists and short story writers
- use evidence from the text.

Key term

Critical responses are those that consider evidence in the text and weigh up different arguments.

Empathic responses are those that show understanding and sympathy for the characters and try to imagine what it would be like to be a character in a text. 'Empathic' comes from the word 'empathy', which means the ability to understand and share the feelings of others.

Tip

In critical essays, evidence from the text should be in the form of brief quotations (or references) which support your points.

Link

You will find more information and guidance on writing answers to empathic questions in Unit 6: 'Developing effective writing skills', on page 143.

Tip

All of the extracts in this Unit have been given line numbers, to make them easy for you to refer to.

As you work through this Unit, you should read the extracts and then do the Activities that follow them.

Responding to characters

From THE HITCH-HIKER
by Roald Dahl

The policeman got off his motorcycle and leaned the machine sideways on to its prop stand. Then he took off his gloves and placed them carefully on the seat. He was in no hurry now. He had us where he wanted us and he knew it.

'This is real trouble,' I said. 'I don't like it one bit.'   5

'Don't talk to 'im any more than is necessary, you understand,' my companion said. 'Just sit tight and keep mum[1].'

1 **keep mum** keep quiet

Like an executioner approaching his victim, the policeman came strolling slowly towards us. He was a big meaty man with a belly, and his blue breeches[2] were skintight around his   10
enormous thighs. His goggles were pulled up on to the helmet, showing a smouldering red face with wide cheeks.

2 **breeches** trousers

We sat there like guilty schoolboys, waiting for him to arrive.

'Watch out for this man,' my passenger whispered. ''Ee looks mean as the devil.'   15

'The policeman came round to my open window and placed one meaty hand on the sill. 'What's the hurry?' he said.

'No hurry, officer,' I answered.

'Perhaps there's a woman in the back having a baby and you're rushing her to hospital? Is that it?'   20

'No, officer.'

'Or perhaps your house is on fire and you're dashing home to rescue the family from upstairs?' His voice was dangerously soft and mocking.

'My house isn't on fire, officer.'   25

'In that case,' he said, 'you've got yourself into a nasty mess, haven't you? Do you know what the speed limit is in this country?'

'Seventy,' I said.

'And do you mind telling me exactly what speed you were   30
doing just now?'

I shrugged and didn't say anything.

When he spoke next, he raised his voice so loud that I jumped.

'One hundred and twenty miles per hour!' he barked. 'That's *fifty* miles an hour over the limit!' 35

He turned his head and spat out a big gob of spit. It landed on the wing of my car and started sliding down over my beautiful blue paint. Then he turned back again and stared hard at my passenger. 'And who are you?' he asked sharply.

'He's a hitch-hiker,' I said. 'I'm giving him a lift.' 40

'I didn't ask you,' he said. 'I asked him.'

''Ave I done somethin' wrong?' my passenger asked. His voice was as soft and oily as haircream.

'That's more than likely,' the policeman answered. 'Anyway, you're a witness. I'll deal with you in a minute. Driving licence,' 45 he snapped, holding out his hand.

I gave him my driving licence.

He unbuttoned the left-hand breast-pocket of his tunic[3] and brought out the dreaded book of tickets. Carefully, he copied the name and address from my licence. Then he gave it back to me. 50 He strolled round to the front of the car and read the number from the numberplate and wrote that down as well. He filled in the date, the time and the details of my offence. Then he tore out the top copy of the ticket. But before handing it to me, he checked that all the information had come through clearly on 55 his own carbon copy. Finally, he replaced the book in his tunic pocket and fastened the button.

'Now you,' he said to my passenger, and he walked around to the other side of the car. From the other breast-pocket he produced a small black notebook. 'Name?' he snapped. 60

3 **tunic** jacket

Exploring the extract from THE HITCH-HIKER by Roald Dahl

This extract from Roald Dahl's **short story** *The Hitch-hiker* features three characters:

- A driver – the character who is telling the story
- A hitch-hiker – the character who speaks with a non-standard English accent
- A policeman.

Prose fiction writers use a variety of methods to bring their characters to life. You will need to consider the following when studying characters in Prose texts:

- What characters do
- What characters think and feel
- What characters say
- What other characters say about them.

Key term

A **short story**, as the name suggests, is shorter than a novel. A short story generally concentrates on a single event and has a small number of main characters.

These are all aspects of **characterisation** – that is, ways in which writers present their characters.

1 Read carefully the extract from *The Hitch-hiker*, paying particular attention to what the character of the policeman says and does.

Look at lines 1–4:

What are your first impressions of the policeman from these two lines?

Write a concise answer of no more than three sentences. Provide evidence from Dahl's writing to support your points.

2 Look at lines 8–12:

Comment on the effects of the words used to describe the policeman. Use a table like the one below to record your answers.

Quotation	Effect of words
Like an executioner approaching his victim	The simile 'like an executioner' suggests how frightening a figure the policeman appeared to the other characters who felt like 'victims'.
strolling slowly towards us	
a big meaty man with a belly	
his blue breeches were skintight around his enormous thighs	
smouldering red face with wide cheeks	

3 Look at lines 19–35:

Consider the way in which the policeman might say the following lines:

- *'Perhaps there's a woman in the back having a baby and you're rushing her to hospital?'*
- *'Is that it?'*
- *'Or perhaps your house is on fire and you're dashing home to rescue the family from upstairs?'*
- *'In that case you've got yourself into a nasty mess, haven't you?'*
- *'And do you mind telling me exactly what speed you were doing just now?'*
- *'One hundred and twenty miles per hour! That's fifty miles an hour over the limit!'*

Key term

Dialogue refers to the words spoken by the characters, in Prose or in Drama.

Link

Consider how the writers handle the mix of story-telling and dialogue in the other extracts in this Unit.

In small groups, practise in turn reading the lines out loud as if you were the policeman. This Activity will help you to match the words to an appropriate tone of voice for the policeman. This in turn will help you develop a clear understanding of:

a the character of the policeman
b the words Dahl uses to present the character.

Prose writers generally mingle description, story-telling and **dialogue** to bring their stories convincingly to life. The amount of each of these ingredients will depend on the story. In this extract, Dahl relies heavily on dialogue – what the characters say.

4 Look at lines 36–46:

Explore the ways in which Dahl conveys the unpleasant nature of the policeman. Think about the following:

a The way he speaks.
b What he does.

Write a paragraph about each, making brief quotations from the extract to support your answers. You could start:

Dahl creates the impression of a man who is terrifying. When he shouts, he makes the driver jump. The verb 'barked' makes him sound like an angry and frightening dog.

5 In what ways does Dahl convey the policeman as a menacing figure in this extract?

You should consider the whole extract when answering this question. Write about 300 words, and use evidence from the extract to support the points you make. You should draw on answers from the earlier Activities.

From SAMPHIRE
by Patrick O'Brian

Sheer, sheer, the white cliff rising, straight up from the sea, so far that the riding waves were nothing but ripples on a huge calm. Up there, unless you leaned over, you did not see them break, but for all the distance the thunder of the water came loud. The wind, too, tearing in from the sea, rushing from a clear, high sky, brought the salt tang of the spray on their lips.

    They were two, standing up there on the very edge of the cliff: they had left the levelled path and come down to the break itself and the man was crouched, leaning over as far as he dared.

5

1 **samphire** fleshy-leaved plant which grows near the sea

Samphire growing on a clifftop. How does this image help you to appreciate the situation in which the husband and wife find themselves in this extract?

2 **as bold as brass** boldly for all to see

'It *is* a clump of samphire[1], Molly,' he said; then louder, half   10
turning, 'Molly, it *is* samphire. I *said* it was samphire, didn't I?'
He had a high, rather unmasculine voice, and he emphasized
his words.

His wife did not reply, although she had heard him the first
time. The round of her chin was trembling like a child's before it   15
cries: there was something in her throat so strong that she could
not have spoken it if it had been for her life.

She stepped a little closer, feeling cautiously for a firm
foothold, and she was right on him and she caught the smell
of his hairy tweed jacket. He straightened so suddenly that he   20
brushed against her. 'Hey look out,' he said, 'I almost trod on
your foot. Yes, it *was* samphire. I said so as soon as I saw it
from down there. Have a look.'

She could not answer, so she knelt and crawled to the edge.
Heights terrified her, always had. She could not close her eyes;   25
that only made it worse. She stared unseeing, while the brilliant
air and the sea and the noise of the sea assaulted her terrified
mind and she clung insanely to the thin grass. Three times
he pointed it out, and the third time she heard him so as to
be able to understand his words. '... fleshy leaves. You see the   30
fleshy leaves? They used them for pickles. Samphire pickles!' He
laughed, excited by the wind, and put his hand on her shoulder.
Even then she writhed away, covering it by getting up and
returning to the path.

He followed her. 'You noted the *fleshy leaves*, didn't you, Molly?   35
They allow the plant to store its nourishment. Like a cactus. Our
native cactus. I *said* it was samphire at once, didn't I, although I have
never actually seen it before. We could almost get it with a stick.'

He was pleased with her for having looked over, and said that
she was coming along very well: she remembered – didn't she? –   40
how he had had to persuade her and persuade her to come up
even the smallest cliff at first, how he had even to be a little
firm. And now there she was going up the highest of them all,
as bold as brass[2]; and it was quite a dangerous cliff too, he said,
with a keen glance out to sea, jutting his chin; but there she was   45
as bold as brass looking over the top of it. He had been quite
right insisting, hadn't he? It was worth it when you were there,
wasn't it? Between these questions he waited for a reply, a 'yes'
or hum of agreement. If he had not insisted she would always
have stayed down there on the beach, wouldn't she? Like a lazy   50
puss. He said, wagging his finger to show that he was not quite

in earnest, that she should always listen to her Lacey (this was a pet name that he had coined for himself). Lacey was her lord and master, wasn't he? Love, honour and obey?

Exploring the extract from SAMPHIRE by Patrick O'Brian

In the extract from Dahl's *The Hitch-hiker*, the dominant voice belonged to the policeman. In *Samphire*, a husband's voice dominates.

Read the extract carefully, paying close attention to the words spoken by the husband and to the reactions of his wife.

6 Look at lines 1–6:

The story opens with a description of the cliff, the sea and the wind.

How effective do you find the following descriptions in view of what happens next? Write a concise sentence on each description.

a *Sheer, sheer, the white cliff rising, straight up from the sea …*
b *… for all the distance the thunder of the water came loud*
c *The wind, too, tearing in from the sea …*

7 Look at lines 10–17:

On a copy of the extract, highlight the following in different colours:

a The words the husband speaks
b The description of his voice and the way he speaks
c The reaction of his wife.

Write down in about 100 words your first impressions of the husband. Use evidence from your highlighted text to support your points.

Use quotation marks to indicate the words you are quoting from the text. For example:

The fact that he 'emphasized his words' shows how fussy and precise he is about the way he speaks.

8 What do you think the following quotations reveal about Molly? Write one or two sentences on each.

His wife did not reply, although she had heard him the first time.

The round of her chin was trembling like a child's before it cries …

She stared unseeing, while the brilliant air and the sea and the noise of the sea assaulted her terrified mind and she clung insanely to the thin grass.

[He] put his hand on her shoulder. Even then she writhed away, covering it by getting up and returning to the path.

9 Look at lines 39–54:

The husband's words are not reported in **direct speech** here, but the writing clearly captures the way the man speaks to his wife.

▶ Using these lines, write out the words you think the husband actually says to his wife. Start with:

> *'I am pleased with you looking over. You are coming along very well. You remember – don't you? – how I had to persuade you …'*

Read aloud your answer, using an appropriate voice for the character. What do you think the words and tone of voice reveal about:

a the character of the man?
b the relationship between the man and his wife?

Use a mind map to record your answer.

You could add your notes to a copy of the examples shown here.

Key term

Direct speech indicates the words actually spoken by the characters. It is usually indicated by the use of inverted commas, or speech marks, around the words the characters speak. For example: 'It is a clump of samphire, Molly,' he said.

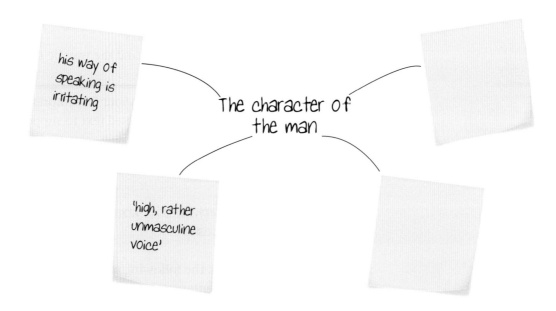

his way of speaking is irritating

The character of the man

'high, rather unmasculine voice'

talks down to
his wife – like
a teacher
rather than
husband

The relationship between
the man and his wife

'You noted the
fleshy leaves,
didn't you,
Molly?'

Tip

Mind maps and tables, such as the ones used in these Activities, can be useful when recording your ideas about the way writers present characters. They are part of an active learning approach to your studies and useful in other subjects as well as Literature.

When using tables, the entries in the 'Comment' column should usually be longer than those in the 'Quotation' column. Remember to keep quotations brief!

Extension

In small groups, work together to produce a script for a radio play, covering lines 35–54 of the extract. Your focus should be on the husband's words and the way the actor speaks them. Next, practise reading the lines exactly as you think the character would say them. Then record the speech.

This Activity can be used for key extracts from any Prose texts you are studying for examination or Coursework. It helps you to consider in detail the writer's use of language and structure.

10 Make a list of *ten* quotations and comments you could use in answering the following question.

Explore the ways in which O'Brian creates sympathy for Molly.

Record your answer in a table like this one.

Quotation	Comment
I said *it was samphire, didn't I?*	Her husband speaks to Molly in a patronising tone, as if she were a child.

From A STRANGER FROM LAGOS
by Cyprian Ekwensi

She saw the way he looked at her when she was dancing and
knew. Only a stranger would look like that at the *Umu-ogbo*
dance, and only a man who had fallen would linger on her
movements that way. Yet it embarrassed her when, sitting with
the elderly women in the bright hot afternoon, she looked up   5
from her sewing and saw him, asking questions. Though she
knew he had seen her, he did not once look in her direction. He
looked so transparently silly and pitiable.

She wondered what to do. Should she go to his help there –
while her mother and her fiancé's mother were present? He   10
seemed to be holding his own, telling fables, something about
having missed his way, having recently crossed the Niger[1] . ...
She would go to his aid. Suddenly she caught the hard look on
his unsmiling face, a look full of the agony of desire.

Her legs felt too heavy to stir. Too many eyes. In Onitsha[2]   15
Town there were eyes on the walls. In the compound, eyes. In
the streets, eyes. Such a small town, and so small-town-minded.
You went down Market Street, new or old, and came back into
Market Street, new or old, through a number of parallel feeder
streets. Of course, Lilian had lived here since she was born and   20
she knew her way to her lover's house without being seen even
by day, and with her mother happily thinking she had gone to
market. But once they saw her, once they saw a girl they knew
and respected speaking with a glamorous-looking stranger like
this one, or in a hotel, or standing in the streets and talking to   25
a *man* in broad daylight, or daring to hold hands or to linger
too long with a handshake, the eyes would roll and the tongues
would wag and the girl's best course of action would be to leave
the town or immediately be branded[3].

By the time Lilian looked up from her machine, he was gone.   30
Her mother was coming back to the veranda.

'What did he say he wanted?'

'Do I know?' Her mother shrugged and made a face. 'These
young men from Lagos, who understands the language they speak?'

Lilian knew he had come for her but his courage had failed him.   35
'Did he say his name, or where he lives?'

'He called a name. He is not of a family I know.'

Unlike her mother, Lilian cared little for 'families she knew'.
She judged young men by what her instincts told her, and this
time they told her she had made a conquest, full of strange   40
enchantment. She put the scissors through the wax print and
shaped it into a skirt that ended well above her knees. Her

1 **Niger** the principal river of western Africa

2 **Onitsha** a city and river port on the eastern part of the Niger in southeastern Nigeria

3 **branded** given a bad reputation

mother's eyes followed her with resentment. She called such
tight clothes 'mad people's clothes'.

On her way down Market Street, Lilian wiggled in the new   45
dress. Her hair had been newly done, and the loop earrings were
large enough to play hula-hoop. Someone stopped just behind
her. She looked round. Eyes. From the windows of the hotels,
bookshops, sign painters, mechanics' workshops, eyes focused
enquiringly on her and the strange with such intentness that she   50
felt like something projected on a 3-D screen for all Onitsha to
view. This was sensation.

He was tall and good-looking and did not show any
embarrassment at being made the spectacle of Market Street. Of
course, he did not know the town. He would scandalise her, and   55
leave her to it. That was the way of strangers. They left you to
the gossips.

'I saw you in the compound – is that where you live?'

'Yes. Please, I am in a hurry. Who are you?'

4 **Lagos** a densely-populated port in
Nigeria

'A stranger from Lagos[4]. If you had time, I would tell you   60
about my mission.'

'Now?' She wrinkled her nose.

'I only stopped because I saw you. It is some days now since I
came to your compound. I have wanted to see you.'

'What for?' she asked unnecessarily. He did not answer.   65
'You're from Lagos?' Lilian said.

'Yes.'

The eyes from the hotels, bookshops, mechanical workshops,
danced. A woman passer-by stopped and greeted Lilian by
name. Lilian seemed to remember the face, and yet she could   70
not place it. Her mind was focused on the stranger. 'How is
your baby?' asked the passer-by. 'How is your mother?' Lilian
mumbled something ...

'You're from Lagos,' Lilian said. 'Here in Onitsha we do not
stop and talk in the streets. It is not considered respectable. It is 75
not done by decent girls of family ... Too many eyes ... Wait till
evening ...

'Till evening, then!'

Exploring the extract from A STRANGER FROM LAGOS by Cyprian Ekwensi

The extract from Patrick O'Brian's story *Samphire* depicted a woman trapped
in a desperately unhappy marriage. This extract from *A Stranger from Lagos*
portrays a woman at odds with the community in which she lives.

How far does this photograph reflect the image of Onitsha that is given in the extract from *A Stranger from Lagos*?

Key term

Narrative is the way in which a story is told. This extract from *A Stranger from Lagos* is the beginning of a short story. The reader is thrown into the middle of the action. There is no introductory paragraph that sets the scene, as in *Samphire*.

Plot refers to the storyline.

⓫ Read the extract carefully, paying close attention to the way the **narrative** develops.

Rearrange the following events in the order they occur in the extract. This Activity will help you to consider the way in which the writer organises the **plot**.

- Lilian walks along Market Street.
- Lilian works at her machine.
- Lilian puts on her new dress and large earrings.
- The stranger meets Lilian at the dance.
- The stranger asks Lilian whether she lives in the compound.

⓬ How effective do you find the first line of the extract? Give reasons for your answer. Write no more than two sentences.

⓭ Look at lines 1–14:

On a copy of the extract, highlight words and phrases that tell us about Lilian's thoughts and feelings. Then annotate the highlighted phrases to show what they reveal about Lilian's thoughts and feelings.

For example:

she thinks he is already in love with her

'only a man who had fallen would linger on her movements that way.'

she knows he's transfixed by her

⓮ Look at lines 15–29:

How do the following quotations help to create a picture of Onitsha and the people who live there?

a *In Onitsha Town there were eyes on the walls.*
b *Such a small town, and so small-town-minded.*
c *… talking to a* man *in broad daylight …*
d *… the eyes would roll and the tongues would wag and the girl's best course of action would be to leave the town or immediately be branded.*

15 Look at lines 15–47:

How do Lilian's values differ from the values of:

a her mother
b the townsfolk?

Highlight on your copy of the extract the brief quotations you would use to answer this question.

Then write two paragraphs, in which you comment on the effects created by the key words in your quotations.

16 Read again lines 47–52:

> *Someone stopped just behind her. She looked round. Eyes. From the windows of the hotels, bookshops, sign painters, mechanics' workshops, eyes focused enquiringly on her and the stranger with such intentness that she felt like something projected on a 3-D screen for all Onitsha to view. This was sensation.*

How do you think the length of each of these five sentences helps to communicate the meaning?

17 Attempt the following empathic question:

You are Lilian. You are waiting to meet the stranger from Lagos again and reflecting on the community in which you live.

Write your thoughts.

Begin by making a concise list of all the points you could use in your answer. Look carefully at Lilian's thoughts and feelings at the particular moment given in the question.

Make sure you stick to the text. You should not introduce new characters or events. Your task is to get into the skin of the character. You should:

- write from Lilian's viewpoint, using the pronoun 'I'
- adopt a voice that is suitable for the character.

Remember that in empathic responses you should use details from the text which help you to develop a convincing voice for the character.

Tip

The values of Lilian contrast with the values of her mother and of the other townsfolk of Onitsha. Stories often revolve around contrasts between characters or between a character and the community they belong to. Such contrasts or differences are useful starting-points for the close study of Prose texts (and also drama texts).

Tip

Good empathic responses capture the authentic voice of the character.

You could start your answer like this:

'It's so difficult for me to walk through the compound and the streets, eyes spying on me everywhere I go ...'

Extension

When you have finished your written response to Activity 17, work in small groups. Each student should read their response in a tone of voice suitable for the character. Others in the group should note the following points from your reading:

- Those phrases which work particularly well for the character
- Those phrases which are less successful.

18 Here are some examples of students' writing for the empathic activity in Activity 17. What do you think is wrong with each of these?

1 If I were Lilian, I would be thinking how hard it was for me to walk down the street unnoticed.

2 I'm so not happy; it's sooo difficult to do anything round here without being seen.

3 My friends and I were on our way to the cinema that evening. We particularly like comedy movies. Then I happened to see a tall, handsome stranger.

Quick recap
Responding to characters

As you study characters in Prose fiction, consider the following questions. Your answers to these questions will help you to acquire a detailed knowledge of the characters in the Prose texts you study. The questions encourage you to appreciate the various ways in which Prose writers present characters.

Five main aspects of a character
- What does a particular character look like?
- What does the character do?
- What does the character say and think?
- What do other characters say and think about the character?
- How does the character develop as the text progresses?

Features of characterisation to explore
- What does the character add to the plot?
- How big a role does the character play in the text?
- How does the writer describe the character's appearance?

Link

You are likely to encounter characters in Prose texts in:

- the Set Texts Papers (Papers 1, 4 and 5)
- the Prose question on the Unseen Paper (Paper 3)
- Prose texts you might study for Coursework.

- How does the writer describe the character's personal qualities?
- Are there deliberate contrasts or conflicts with other characters?
- Is the character at odds with the society in which they live?
- In what ways does the writer convey a distinctive voice for the character?

Active learning strategies

It is recommended that you try one or more of the following strategies to improve your appreciation of characters and the way they are presented in stories:

- Highlight and annotate key words
- List points
- Use 'Quotation + Comment' tables
- Write a summary
- Draw mind maps
- Write notes from the character's viewpoint
- Record key lines spoken by the character

Tip

For the Prose text you study for the Set Texts Paper, you could include examples of all these active learning strategies for each of the major characters.

Responding to setting and mood

From THE SIEGE
by Helen Dunmore

It is hard work walking through the snow. Already, after a few hundred metres, Anna's heart is thudding painfully. She stops to cough. She's out of breath, and a sweat of weakness starts out over her body, trickling between her shoulder-blades. She ought to have tried harder to get hold of some horehound pastilles[1] for this cough, which has been dragging on for two weeks now. But when they get a stove, everything will be better.   5

Because she can't walk fast, she isn't keeping warm. Usually her blood seems to flow more brightly in winter. She's buoyant, glowing, always the one who stays in the park long after dusk,   10
hauling children up slopes on their sledge. Winter suits her. Her eyes are bright, her skin clear, her lips red. More than anything she loves winter nights, with their scent of tangerines and frost, and the staring brilliance of stars. But today the snow is oppressive. Anna's not sure that she's moving forward.   15
Perhaps only the veil of falling snow is moving and she herself is treading in the same footprints, over and over again.

She forces herself on. She's so hungry. Somehow the hunger feels sharper out here. Indoors, you become torpid[2]. You're weak, but you don't understand quite how weak until you try to do   20
something which demands energy. You move slowly, and rest a lot,

1 **horehound pastilles** cough medicine made from a plant

2 **torpid** mentally or physically inactive

like an invalid. You take time to build up to making tea, and lean against the table while the water boils. Hours drift past, glazed.

But out here it's frightening. She mustn't rest, not even for a minute, or the cold will get her. Even though there's no wind, the snow seems to be pushing her backwards.   25

Across the street she sees Klavdia from the nursery laundry, dragging a heavy canvas sack. But Klavdia's eyes stare blankly, or even with hostility, and Anna's greeting dies in her mouth. Was it really Klavdia, or just someone who looked like her? Or   30
perhaps there was no one there at all. You can easily imagine things. Sometimes grains of blackness thicken in front of her eyes. A cluster of falling flakes takes on the shape of a face. At the corner, snow devils are dancing, in spite of the lack of wind.

Heads down, scattered on the white streets like flakes of soot, a few figures fight their way onward. If she collapsed, no   35
one would be able to help her. No one has the strength. It's hard enough to survive, to get the bread ration, to fetch water if you're in an apartment where the pipes have already frozen, to toil from empty shop to empty shop in search of milk for a sick child.   40

'But I'm fine,' Anna says aloud, and tastes a flake of snow on her lips. It's only being alone in the snow that makes her nervous. Her heart's beating so hard. If only she had some valerian drops[3], to calm herself. Even though the snow is moving, and she is moving, it's all like an icy dream from which   45
life has fled. She could look down on herself and watch herself struggling on, an insect which doesn't know that it's winter and it shouldn't be out. It's quite funny, when you look down on yourself like that.

3 **valerian drops** medicine made from the valerian plant

Leningrad (now St Petersburg) during the siege of 1941.

Exploring the extract from THE SIEGE by Helen Dunmore

Setting refers to where the action takes place. It is where the characters' thoughts, words and actions are situated. There may be more than one setting in the novel or short story. And a particular setting may change as the story progresses.

The setting in this passage from *The Seige* is very bleak. The character struggles heroically against a formidable enemy: the weather.

Tense refers to the form of a verb, which shows the time when an action happened. For example, 'She stopped' is past tense, so the action of stopping occurred in the past; 'She stops' is the present tense, where the action is taking place now.

This extract is from Helen Dunmore's novel *The Siege* set in 1941 in the city of Leningrad (now called St Petersburg), at a time when the citizens endured starvation and a merciless Russian winter. The German tanks surrounding the city meant that it was under siege and no food could get through to the city. The description of the snow and the main character's struggle with it help to create a vivid picture of the **setting**.

You will notice that there is no dialogue in this extract.

19 Read the extract carefully.

Look at lines 1–17:

In what ways does Dunmore convey the physical effects of the cold and snow on Anna?

On a copy of the extract, highlight the key words and add brief annotations in the margin. Your annotations should comment precisely on the effects of particular words or phrases.

20 Look at lines 1–7:

a Re-write the first paragraph using the past **tense**.
b Why do you think Dunmore uses the present tense to describe Anna's trudging through the snow?
   Write a brief paragraph, using references to the text to support your answer.

21 Look at lines 18–23:

Consider the effects created by using the following:

a short sentences
b the pronoun 'You'.

22 Look at lines 24–33:

How does Dunmore depict the way in which Anna battles with the weather?

Use a table like this to record material which is useful for your answer.

Quotation	Comment
'... or the cold will get her'	The personification of the cold here creates the impression of a predator waiting for its prey the moment she rests.

23 Look at lines 46–49:

How effective do you find these final two sentences of the extract?

She could look down on herself and watch herself struggling on, an insect which doesn't know that it's winter and it shouldn't be out. It's quite funny, when you look down on yourself like that.

Write a paragraph in which you comment on:

a what you understand by the 'insect' metaphor used here
b Anna's feelings about herself at this moment.

From THE LEMON ORCHARD
by Alex La Guma

The men came down between two long, regular rows of trees. The winter had not passed completely and there was a chill in the air; and the moon was hidden behind long, high parallels of cloud which hung like suspended streamers of dirty cotton wool in the sky. All of the men but one wore thick clothes against the   5
coolness of the night. The night and earth was cold and damp, and the shoes of the men sank into the soil and left exact, ridged foot prints, but they could not be seen in the dark.

One of the men walked ahead holding a small cycle lantern that worked from a battery, leading the way down the avenue of   10
trees while the others came behind in the dark. The night close around was quiet now that the crickets had stopped their small noises, but far out others that did not feel the presence of the men continued the monotonous creek-creek-creek. Somewhere, even further, a dog started barking in short high yaps, and then   15
stopped abruptly. The men were walking through an orchard of lemons and the sharp, bitter-sweet citrus smell hung gently on the night air.

'Do not go so fast,' the man who brought up the rear of the party called to the man with the lantern. 'It's dark as a kaffir's[1]   20
soul here at the back.'

He called softly, as if the darkness demanded silence. He was a big man and wore khaki trousers and laced-up riding boots, and an old shooting jacket with leather patches on the right breast and the elbows.   25

The shotgun was loaded. In the dark this man's face was invisible except for a blur of shadowed hollows and lighter crags. Although he walked in the rear he was the leader of the party. The lantern-bearer slowed down for the rest to catch up with him.

'It's cold, too, Oom,' another man said.   30

1 **kaffir** an offensive term in Southern Africa for a black person

2 **verdomte** a swear word

3 **hotnot** bushman (from 'hottentot', an offensive term for black people once used in Southern Africa)

'Cold?' the man with the shotgun asked, speaking with sarcasm. 'Are you colder than this verdomte[2] hotnot[3], here?' And he gestured in the dark with the muzzle of the gun at the man who stumbled along in their midst and who was the only one not warmly dressed.

This man wore trousers and a raincoat which they had allowed him to pull on over his pyjamas when they had taken him from his lodgings, and he shivered now with the chill, clenching his teeth to prevent then from chattering. He had not been given time to tie his shoes and the metal-covered ends of the laces clicked as he moved. 35

40

'Are you cold, hotnot?' the man with the light jeered.

The coloured man did not reply. He was afraid, but his fear was mixed with a stubbornness which forbade him to answer them.

'He is not cold,' the fifth man in the party said. 'He is shivering with fear. It is not so, hotnot?' 45

The coloured man said nothing, but stared ahead of himself into the half-light made by the small lantern. He could see the silhouette of the man who carried the light, but he did not want to look at the two who flanked him, the one who had complained of the cold, and the one who had spoken of his fear. 50

4 **sjambok** whip

5 **corduroyed** ribbed cotton

They each carried a sjambok[4] and every now and then one of them slapped a corduroyed[5] leg with his.

'He is dumb also,' the one who had spoken last chuckled.

'No, Andries. Wait a minute,' the leader who carried the shotgun said, and they all stopped between the row of trees. The man with the lantern turned and put the light on the rest of the party. 55

'What is it?' he asked.

6 **Wag'n oomblikkie** 'Wait a moment' (in Afrikaans, a Southern African language)

7 **baas** white boss

8 **riem** rawhide strap or belt

'Wag'n oomblikkie[6]. Wait a moment,' the leader said, speaking with forced casualness. 'He is not dumb. He is a slim hotnot; one of those educated bushmen. Listen, hotnot,' he addressed the coloured man, speaking angrily now. 'When a baas[7] speaks to you, you answer him. Do you hear?' The coloured man's wrists were tied behind him with a riem[8] and the leader brought the muzzle of the shotgun down, pressing it hard into the small of the man's back above where the wrists met. 'Do you hear, hotnot? Answer me or I will shoot a hole through your spine.' 60

65

The bound man felt the hard round metal of the gun muzzle through the loose raincoat and clenched his teeth. He was cold and tried to prevent himself from shivering in case it should be mistaken for cowardice. He heard the small metallic noise as the man with the gun thumbed back the hammer of the shotgun. In spite of the cold little drops of sweat began to form on his upper lip under the overnight stubble. 70

'For God's sake, don't shoot him,' the man with the light said, laughing a little nervously. 'We don't want to be involved in any murder.' 75

Exploring the extract from THE LEMON ORCHARD by Alex La Guma

The extract from *The Siege* showed the interaction between character and setting, namely Anna battling against the bleak and cold backdrop of Leningrad in winter. This extract from *The Lemon Orchard* is from the beginning of a short story. The setting is as mysterious as the action narrated in the story.

Key term

Mood is created by writers through their use of description and dialogue. Another word for mood is 'atmosphere'. La Guma uses description in his first two paragraphs and dialogue in his third to convey a particular mood or atmosphere.

Senses are what enable us to experience the world around us. Writers often use language which appeals to our senses of sight, hearing, touch, smell and taste. They do this to make their writing come alive for the reader.

24 Read the extract carefully.

Look at lines 1–8.

The story begins mysteriously. Write one sentence about each of the following phrases, explaining how they help to create a mysterious and menacing **mood**.

1 *there was a chill in the air*
2 *the moon was hidden*
3 *cloud which hung like suspended streamers of dirty cotton wool*
4 *The night and earth was cold and damp*
5 *exact, ridged footprints … could not be seen in the dark*

Tip

Writers often use descriptions which appeal to the senses: sight, hearing, smell, taste and touch. Close study of where such descriptions occur in a text can help you to enter more fully the imaginative world created by the writer.

25 Look at lines 9–18:

In order to bring the setting to life, La Guma uses description which appeals to the **senses**. List in a table like this the senses he uses, together with examples from this paragraph.

Sense	Example
Sight	small cycle lantern

26 Look at lines 19–34.

Consider both the speech and description of the leader of the men. What impressions do you form of him here? Refer closely to the text to support your views. Remember to use quotation marks around any words and phrases you quote from the extract.

Link

Re-read the extracts from *Samphire* and *The Siege* to discover how these writers too appeal to the senses in their writing.

27 Re-read the whole extract from *The Lemon Orchard*. How do you think La Guma creates sympathy for the captive man in the story?

First, use a table like the one at the top of the next page to help with your gathering of evidence to answer the question. As in the example, your entries should be longer in the 'Comment on language' column than in the 'Quotation' column.

Quotation	Comment on language
the only one not warmly dressed	This description stresses the isolation of this particular man. The reader is intrigued as to why he is not as warmly dressed as the others on a cold night.

Then write an answer to the question above in about 250 words. Include quotations and analytical comment to support your points.

28 The plot of the story is what happens on the surface of the text. The **theme** (or themes) of the story refer to what the story is about at a deeper level.

Which of the statements below relate to the plot of *The Lemon Orchard*?

Which statements relate to themes?

Record your answers in a table like this.

Plot	Theme
	The story concerns the effects of racism

- An inadequately-dressed man is marched from his home against his will.
- Some of the men jeered at the captive man.
- The story concerns the effects of racism.
- The leader of the men threatened the captive by pressing his gun into the captive's back.
- The story is about one man's isolation and sense of powerlessness.

Quick recap
Responding to setting and mood

Writers take great care when creating settings and mood. Remember: there may well be more than one setting in a text, and the mood is likely to change as the novel or story progresses.

The following checklist will help you to appreciate more fully both the setting and mood of a text. You could use this checklist for relevant pages of the Prose texts you are studying.

Five key questions for exploring setting
- Which key words are used to describe the setting?
- Is the setting described in physical terms?

Tip

Long quotations should be avoided. They simply show that you can copy from a text. In your critical essays, you should use brief quotations from texts as a starting-point for your close analysis. The examiner is interested in your views about *why* the writer has used particular words and phrases. You need to focus on the effects created by the writer's deliberate choices.

Key term

Theme is the word used to explain the deeper meanings of the story. Themes which are common in literature are childhood, love, conflict, war, the passage of time, death, ambition, deception, and the list goes on.

Tip

Reading Harper Lee's novel *To Kill a Mockingbird* provides a powerful insight into racism in the American Deep South during the 1930s. But you would not receive credit for writing generally about racism or more specifically about 1930s attitudes towards race. Nor would you receive credit for writing details of Lee's life. Your key focus in Literature must be the text and how the writer explores themes such as racism *within the text itself.*

Tip

You should make notes on the key settings and moods for the Prose texts you study. Mind maps are useful in collating the relevant material.

- Does the writer use language which appeals to particular senses?
- In what ways do characters interact with the setting?
- Does the setting represent an aspect of the theme(s)?

Five questions for exploring mood

- Which key words are used to capture a particular mood?
- How is description used to convey mood?
- How does dialogue contribute to the mood?
- Are there any clear shifts in the mood?
- Where and why do the shifts in mood occur?

Responding to narrative viewpoint

From STUDIES IN THE PARK
by Anita Desai

— Turn it off, turn if off, turn it off! First he listens to the news in Hindi. Directly after, in English. Broom – brroom – brrroom – the voice of doom roars. Next, in Tamil. Then in Punjabi. In Gujarati. What next, my god, what next? Turn it off before I smash it onto his head, fling it out of the window, do nothing of   5
the sort of course, nothing of the sort.

— And my mother. She cuts and fries, cuts and fries. All day I hear her chopping and slicing and the pan of oil hissing. What all does she find to fry and feed us on, for God's sake? Eggplants, potatoes, spinach, shoe soles, newspapers, finally   10
she'll slice me and feed me to my brothers and sisters. Ah, now she's turned on the tap. It's roaring and pouring, pouring and roaring into a bucket without a bottom.

— The bell rings. Voices clash, clatter and break. The tin-and-bottle man? The neighbours? The Police? The Help-the-   15
Blind man? Thieves and burglars? All of them, all of them, ten or twenty or a hundred of them, marching up the stairs, hammering at the door, breaking in and climbing over me – ten, twenty or a hundred of them.

— Then, worst of all, the milk arrives. In the tallest glass in the   20
house. 'Suno, drink your milk. Good for you, Suno. You need it. Now, before the exams. Must have it, Suno. Drink.' The voice wheedles[1] its way into my ear like a worm. I shudder. The table tips over. The milk runs. The tumbler clangs on the floor. 'Suno, Suno, how will you do your exams?'   25

1 **wheedles** tempts by soft words

2 **pilgrimage to Hardwar** journey
to an Indian city

— That is precisely what I ask myself. All very well to give me
a room – Uncle's been pushed off on a pilgrimage to Hardwar[2]
to clear a room for me – and to bring me milk and say, 'Study,
Suno, study for your exam.' What about the uproar around
me? These people don't know the meaning of the word Quiet. 30
When my mother fills buckets, sloshes the kitchen floor, fries
and sizzles things in the pan, she thinks she is being Quiet. The
children have never even heard the word, it amazes and puzzles
them. On their way back from school they fling their satchels
in at my door, then tear in to snatch them back before I tear 35
them to bits. Bawl when I pull their ears, screech when mother
whacks them. Stuff themselves with her fries and then smear
the grease on my books.

So I raced out of my room, with my fingers in my ears, to
scream till the roof fell down about their ears. But the radio 40
suddenly went off, the door to my parents' room suddenly
opened and my father appeared, bathed and shaven, stuffed and
set up with the news of the world in six different languages – his
white *dhoti*[3] blazing, his white shirt crackling, his patent leather
pumps glittering. He stopped in the doorway and I stopped on 45
the balls of my feet and wavered. My fingers came out of my
ears, my hair came down over my eyes. Then he looked away
from me, took his watch out of his pocket and enquired, 'Is
the food ready?' in a voice that came out of his nose like the
whistle of a punctual train. He skated off towards his meal, 50
I turned and slouched back to my room. On his way to work, he
looked in to say, 'Remember, Suno. I expect good results from
you. Study hard, Suno.' Just behind him, I saw all the rest of
them standing, peering in, silently. All of them stared at me, at
the exam I was to take. At the degree I was to get. Or not to get. 55
Horrifying thought. Oh study, study, study, they all breathed at
me while my father's footsteps went down the stairs, crushing
each underfoot in turn. I felt their eyes on me, goggling, and
their breath on me, hot with earnestness[4]. I looked back at
them, into their open mouths and staring eyes. 60

'Study,' I said, and found I croaked. 'I know I ought to study.
And how do you expect me to study – in this madhouse? You
run wild, *wild*. I'm getting out,' I screamed, leaping up and
grabbing my books, 'I'm going to study outside. Even the street
is quieter,' I screeched and threw myself past them and down 65
the stairs that my father had just cowed and subjugated so that
they still lay quivering, and paid no attention to the howls that
broke out behind me of 'Suno, Suno, listen. Your milk – your
studies – your exams, Suno!'

3 **dhoti** traditional Indian dress
for men
4 **earnestness** seriousness

This student finds the peace and quiet
denied to the narrator in the extract.

77

Key term

The **narrator** is the person who tells the story in a novel or short story. What happens is told through their words.

A **first person narrator** is an actual character in the novel. All the events of the novel are told through this character. We see events and other characters through their eyes. First person narrators can communicate:

- what they themselves think
- what they themselves have heard
- what others have told them.

Stream of consciousness is a particular technique Prose writers can use to convey a person's mind as it moves from thought to thought. The effect is rather like being able to listen to a character's thoughts in real time.

Exploring the extract from STUDIES IN THE PARK by Anita Desai

A **narrator** is the person who tells a story. This story makes use of a **first person narrator.** In this case, events are seen through the eyes of a student who is desperate to study in peace, away from the distraction of noise. The viewpoint is provided by the narrator.

29 Read the extract carefully.

Write a short paragraph explaining why the first sentence makes an effective opening to the story.

30 As you read the passage, what impressions do you form of the narrator and his attitude towards his family?

Write about 200 words, referring to details in the text to support your points.

31 Desai uses **stream of consciousness** writing to capture vividly the boy's thoughts and feelings. Remember that writers make deliberate choices about the language they use.

Use one copy of the extract to highlight examples of the following sound devices:

- Alliteration
- Assonance
- Onomatopoeia
- Rhyme.

Annotate the examples with concise analytical comments on the effects Desai creates by using these specific devices.

32 Use a second copy of the extract to highlight examples of the following devices:

- Imagery
- Rhetorical question
- Hyperbole
- Humour.

Annotate these examples with concise analytical comments on the effects created by the use of these devices.

Tip

Remember that literary terms such as the ones used in Activities 31 and 32 can be useful, but they are only a starting-point for analysis. You should not merely list or describe devices used by writers. You need to comment on *how* writers use words to create particular effects. The quality of your analytical comment is more important than being able to simply spot particular literary devices.

Tip

Activities 31 and 32 require you to highlight words and phrases on copies of the extract. Adopt a disciplined approach to 'highlighting' words. You could use one or more of the following methods:

- Colour highlighting (with a highlighter pen)
- Underlining words
- Circling words
- Drawing a box around words
- Putting an abbreviation near a word (e.g. 'O' for onomatopoeia).

1 **vaunt** boast

2 **fancied** imagined

33 Write a response to the following question, in about 300 words:

What impressions do you form of the narrator as you read the passage?

Remember to use quotations and to analyse the effects of particular words and sounds.

 Further reading

The following novels make distinctive use of first person narrators. Choose two of these books, by different authors. You may not have time to read the whole book, but try reading one or two chapters, to get an idea of the narrative voice each of the writers uses, and compare them.

Great Expectations by Charles Dickens
The Catcher in the Rye by J.D. Salinger
To Kill a Mockingbird by Harper Lee
The God Boy by Ian Cross
Crick Crack, Monkey by Merle Hodge
The Curious Incident of the Dog in the Night-time by Mark Haddon
Purple Hibiscus by Chimamanda Ngozi Adichie

From HARD TIMES by Charles Dickens

He was a rich man: banker, merchant, manufacturer, and what not. A big, loud man, with a stare, and a metallic laugh. A man made out of a coarse material, which seemed to have been stretched to make so much of him. A man with a great puffed head and forehead, swelled veins in his temples, and such a strained skin to his face that it seemed to hold his eyes open, and lift his eyebrows up. A man with a pervading appearance on him of being inflated like a balloon, and ready to start. A man who could never sufficiently vaunt[1] himself a self-made man. A man who was always proclaiming, through that brassy speaking-trumpet of a voice of his, his old ignorance and his old poverty. A man who was the Bully of humility.

A year or two younger than his eminently practical friend, Mr. Bounderby looked older; his seven or eight and forty might have had the seven or eight added to it again, without surprising anybody. He had not much hair. One might have fancied[2] he had talked it off; and that what was left, all standing up in disorder, was in that condition from being constantly blown about by his windy boastfulness.

5

10

15

3 **mortar** mixture of cement, sand
and water used to bond bricks

4 **physic** medicine
5 **inflammation** swelling
6 **imbecility** stupidity

How does this illustration add to
your appreciation of the character of
Mr Bounderby?

A **third person narrator**
is often referred to as an
omniscient (or all-knowing)
narrator. This type of narrator
is able to comment on
everything that all characters
say, think and do.

In the formal drawing-room of Stone Lodge, standing on the   20
hearthrug, warming himself before the fire, Mr. Bounderby
delivered some observations to Mrs. Gradgrind on the
circumstance of its being his birthday. He stood before the fire,
partly because it was a cool spring afternoon, though the sun
shone; partly because the shade of Stone Lodge was always   25
haunted by the ghost of damp mortar[3]; partly because he thus took
up a commanding position, from which to subdue Mrs. Gradgrind.

'I hadn't a shoe to my foot. As to a stocking, I didn't know
such a thing by name. I passed the day in a ditch, and the night
in a pigsty. That's the way I spent my tenth birthday. Not that a ditch   30
was new to me, for I was born in a ditch.'

Mrs. Gradgrind, a little, thin, white, pink-eyed bundle of
shawls, of surpassing feebleness, mental and bodily; who was
always taking physic[4] without any effect, and who, whenever
she showed a symptom of coming to life, was invariably stunned   35
by some weighty piece of fact tumbling on her; Mrs. Gradgrind
hoped it was a dry ditch?

'No! As wet as a sop. A foot of water in it,' said Mr. Bounderby.

'Enough to give a baby cold,' Mrs. Gradgrind considered.

'Cold? I was born with inflammation[5] of the lungs, and of   40
everything else, I believe, that was capable of inflammation,'
returned Mr. Bounderby. 'For years, ma'am, I was one of the
most miserable little wretches ever seen. I was so sickly, that I
was always moaning and groaning. I was so ragged and dirty,
that you wouldn't have touched me with a pair of tongs.'   45

Mrs. Gradgrind faintly looked at the tongs, as the most
appropriate thing her imbecility[6] could think of doing.

'How I fought through it, *I* don't know,' said Bounderby. 'I was
determined, I suppose. I have been a determined character in
later life, and I suppose I was then. Here I am, Mrs. Gradgrind,   50
anyhow, and nobody to thank for my being here, but myself.'

Exploring the extract from HARD TIMES by Charles Dickens

In this extract, a **third person narrator** introduces the character
Mr Bounderby.

34 What does the narrator reveal about Bounderby? Write your answer
under the following headings:

- His childhood
- His position in society
- His appearance
- His effect on Mrs Gradgrind.

35 How does Dickens use dialogue to convey Bounderby's character?

Write about 200 words, referring to the detail of the extract in answering the question.

36 Look at line 36 to the end of the extract.

Re-write this part of the extract from Mrs Gradgrind's viewpoint. Write about 200 words in character, using first person narration.

You could begin in this way:

I said, 'Mr Bounderby, I hope the ditch was a dry ditch.'
   'No! As wet as a sop. A foot of water in it,' he replied.
   'Enough to give a baby a cold,' I ventured.

37 In small groups, read aloud your answers to Activity 36. Using the questions below, discuss the differences between your first person narration and Dickens' original third person narration.

a What are the benefits of third person narration?
b What are the disadvantages of third person narration?
c What are the benefits of presenting the narrative from Mrs Gradgrind's viewpoint?
d What are the disadvantages of presenting the narrative from Mrs Gradgrind's viewpoint.

From ETHAN FROME
by Edith Wharton

I had the story, bit by bit, from various people and, as generally happens in such cases, each time it was a different story.

   If you know Starkfield, Massachusetts, you know the post-office. If you know the post-office you must have seen Ethan Frome drive up to it, drop the reins on his hollow-backed bay[1] and drag himself across the brick pavement to the white   5
colonnade: and you must have asked who he was.

   It was there that, several years ago, I saw him for the first time; and the sight pulled me up sharp. Even then he was the most striking figure in Starkfield, though he was but the ruin   10
of a man. It was not so much his great height that marked him, for the 'natives' were easily singled out by their lank longitude from the stockier foreign breed: it was the careless powerful look he had, in spite of a lameness checking each step like the jerk of a chain. There was something bleak and unapproachable   15

1 **bay** horse

2 **trolley** tramcar

in his face, and he was so stiffened and grizzled that I took him
for an old man and was surprised to hear that he was not more
than fifty-two. I had this from Harmon Gow, who had driven
the stage from Bettsbridge to Starkfield in pre-trolley[2] days and
knew the chronicle of all the families on his line.   20

'He's looked that way ever since he had his smash-up; and
that's twenty-four years ago come next February,' Harmon threw
out between reminiscent pauses.

The 'smash-up' it was – I gathered from the same informant –
which, besides drawing the red gash across Ethan Frome's   25
forehead, had so shortened and warped his right side that it
cost him a visible effort to take the few steps from his buggy to
the post-office window. He used to drive in from his farm every
day at about noon, and as that was my own hour for fetching
my mail I often passed him in the porch or stood beside him   30
while we waited on the motions of the distributing hand behind
the grating. I noticed that, though he came so punctually, he
seldom received anything but a copy of the *Bettsbridge Eagle*,
which he put without a glance into his sagging pocket. At
intervals, however, the post-master would hand him an envelope   35
addressed to Mrs Zenobia – or Mrs Zeena-Frome, and usually
bearing conspicuously in the upper left-hand corner the address
of some manufacturer of patent medicine and the name of his

3 **specific** medicine

specific[3]. These documents my neighbour would also pocket
without a glance, as if too much used to them to wonder at their   40
number and variety, and would then turn away with a silent nod
to the post-master.

4 **mien** appearance
5 **taciturnity** quietness

Everyone in Starkfield knew him and gave him a greeting
tempered to his own grave mien[4]; but his taciturnity[5] was
respected and it was only on rare occasions that one of the older 45
men of the place detained him for a word. When this happened
he would listen quietly, his blue eyes on the speaker's face, and
answer in so low a tone that his words never reached me; then
he would climb stiffly into his buggy, gather up the reins in his
left hand and drive slowly away in the direction of his farm.   50

'It was a pretty bad smash-up?' I questioned Harmon, looking
after Frome's retreating figure, and thinking how gallantly his
lean brown head, with its shock of light hair, must have sat on
his strong shoulders before they were bent out of shape.

6 **Wust** worst

'Wust[6] kind,' my informant assented. 'More'n enough to kill   55
most men. But the Fromes are tough. Ethan'll likely touch a
hundred.'

'Good God!' I exclaimed. At the moment Ethan Frome, after
climbing to his seat, had leaned over to assure himself of the
security of a wooden box – also with a druggist's label on it –   60

which he had placed in the back of the buggy, and I saw his face as it probably looked when he thought himself alone. "*That* man touch a hundred? He looks as if he was dead and in hell now!"

How does this image of Ethan Frome, taken from a film of the novel, made in 1993, compare with the image you get of Ethan from reading this extract?

Exploring the extract from ETHAN FROME by Edith Wharton

Writers can sequence events chronologically (in the order they happened), or they can arrange the events in a different order. In this extract, from the beginning of the novel, the first person narrator attempts to piece together bits of Ethan Frome's life story.

38 Read the extract carefully. Look at lines 3–6.

How effective do you find the repeated use of 'You'?

Answer concisely, giving reasons for your answer.

39 What do you learn of Starkfield in this extract, and the narrator's attitude towards it?

Write one paragraph for your answer, quoting and commenting on relevant details from the extract.

Tip

Many writers of Prose fiction take great care over the way in which they sequence their material. In this case, Wharton reveals information about Ethan Frome in a way that intrigues the reader. Questions are raised in the reader's mind that will be answered during the course of the novel.

40 On a copy of the extract, highlight all references to time. Start with 'several years ago' (line 8).

Then use a mind map with the words 'Information about Ethan' in the centre. Set out concisely the pieces of information the narrator gives about Ethan, in the order they are given.

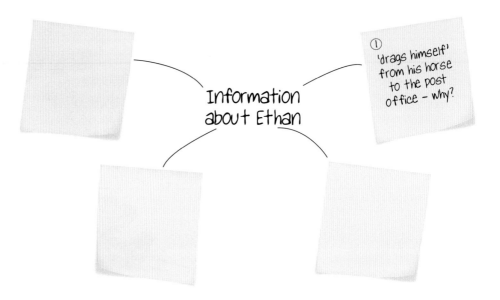

① 'drags himself' from his horse to the post office – why?

Information about Ethan

41 Wharton provides information piece by piece so that we build a picture of Ethan in our heads gradually.

Write about 200 words in response to the following question:

How does Wharton sequence for maximum impact the pieces of information she gives us about Ethan?

42 Using your answers to the previous Activities on this extract, write a response to the following question in about 300 words.

In what ways does Wharton make this such an intriguing opening to the novel?

In your answer, write about the way Wharton:

* creates the setting of Starkfield
* presents details about Ethan's life
* introduces aspects of his wife Zeena's character
* uses first person narration.

Quick recap

Responding to narrative viewpoint

A very important question for readers of Prose fiction is 'Who is telling the story?'

The following checklist will help you to consider the role of the narrator.

First person narrator
- Who is the narrator?
- What is their relationship with other characters?
- Who and what do they approve and disapprove of?
- What information can they reveal?
- Is the narrator reliable or unreliable?

Third person narrator
- Who do they approve and disapprove of?
- Do they provide explicit judgements about other characters?
- What information can they reveal?
- Do they identify closely with a particular character?

Handling of time
- Do they sequence events chronologically?
- Or do they arrange events in a non-chronological order?
- Is information deliberately withheld or left vague until explained later in the text?

Tip

First person narrators have the status of actual characters who happen to guide our responses to other characters and events.

Third person narrators are omniscient: they can reveal what all characters say or think. They can be everywhere at once. However, it is possible for a third person narrator to identify closely with a particular character.

Developing an informed personal response to a complete short story

Read the following complete short story, and then do the Activities which follow.

THE PIECES OF SILVER
by Karl Sealy

When, at five minutes to ten, the bell started to ring, a pall of silence settled over the noisy playfield.

Reluctantly games of cricket and pick-ups were abandoned; climbers came slithering down from the old tamarind tree on the school grounds or dropped quickly from its branches, making haste to clear their mouths of the green, acid fruit they had been enjoying.

5

The school of four hundred-odd boys assembled in ranks across the pebbled playfield, waiting for inspection before they could file into the red-walled school. Some glanced apprehensively at their dusty, naked feet, while others tried feverishly to make their nails and hands presentable. 10

The teachers came from the schoolroom in a leisurely bunch, laughing and joking in quiet voices as they sauntered[1] towards the boys. 15

The stout, pompous, acting Headmaster came to the window that opened off his platform on to the playfield, still making an unnecessary clangour with his bell, and looked sternly over the assembled rows of scholars. The smaller boys straightened and stiffened under his cold gaze. 20

As the teachers passed slowly along the ranks the boys turned their hands back and forth and grinned to show their teeth. A number of boys who failed to pass the teachers' inspection of health were hauled out of the ranks and ordered in to the acting Head. There were three strokes with his cane of plaited tamarind stalks for unclean hands; four for improperly brushed teeth and six for an uncombed head. 25

After the inspection the boys filed quietly into school and to their different classes. When you could have heard a pin drop the schoolmaster rapped out the order: 'Shun!'[2] The entire school of boys flung their hands to their foreheads and chanted: 'Good morning to our teachers.' 30

The schoolmaster announced a hymn and emitting an untrue, faltering note, invited the scholars to take it. The boys rendered a rich improvement of the sound, and when the schoolmaster flung his hand up and stamped his foot they tore full-throatedly into the hymn. 35

At the conclusion of the hymn, the boys sang, 'Amen,' bringing their hands up to their faces in an attitude of prayer. The schoolmaster submitted a long, impromptu supplication[3], rambling and ill-worded, at the end of which the boys said 'Amen' once more. Again the schoolmaster ordered: 'Shun!' The boys came to attention, and school was ready to begin. 40

But this morning the schoolmaster did not order the school to be seated as was the normal custom after prayers. Instead he fixed the school with cold eyes and said: 45

'Those that have brought contributions to Mr Megahey's purse will give them to their teachers.'

Hands delved into pockets, while, in the lower classes, a number of small, moist fists closed still more tightly over the pieces of silver which had been wrapped in paper and pressed carefully into their palms. 50

1 **sauntered** walked in a leisurely manner

2 **shun!** (short for) 'Attention!'

3 **impromptu supplication** prayer spoken without preparation

The teachers drew chairs and stools to their respective desks and sat down. Each produced a foolscap sheet on which were recorded the names of those of his class who had contributed to the purse for the retiring Head, Mr Megahey. 55

4 **commendation** prayer

No commendation[4] seemed due to the donor of three pence. A sixpence was held up between the thumb and forefinger of the receiving teacher and displayed before the class, while the name of the boy who had presented it was repeated some half a dozen times. Still more ado was made of the bestower[5] of a shilling. In addition to being patted on the shoulder and beamed on by his teacher, and basking in the envy of his class, he was sent up to be thanked by the acting Head who shook his hand heartily and showed the gleaming gold of his teeth, and who, with a grave gesture, bestowed upon him the fag-end of a stick of chalk with the injunction that it be not used about the school. 60 / 65

5 **bestower** giver

The receipt of the contributions was over, and the last boy had returned to his seat. On the platform the acting Head cleared his throat for attention and said: 70

'Those who have contributed to our retiring head's purse will now sit. Those who have *not* will remain standing.'

6 **tumult** confused noise

When the scuffling tumult[6] of a school of boys taking their seats had subsided, here and there about the schoolroom a scattered few stood with downcast eyes. 75

The acting Head was a squat jug of a man, fierce-eyed and unsmiling. He now sauntered along the edge of his platform and fixed, one after the other, each of the standing boys with a look of complete scorn. Then, mopping his brow, he ordered those who had brought no gifts to come up and mount the platform where the dozen of them were lined up. 80

Taking a stick of chalk he scrawled an X upon the forehead of each boy, to the huge delight of the rest of the school. When he had imprinted this symbol of shame upon the brow of each unhappy child, he turned to the laughing school, and holding his hand up to check the gusts of merriment, said: 85

'Look! They bear the symbol of ingratitude!'

The cruel laughter went up to the rafters. The schoolmaster permitted it free swell for a few moments before raising his hand once more. 90

'Ingratitude,' he went on, 'ingratitude, more strong than human hand … Come, Clement. You're in the fourth. Step forward and let's hear Mark Antony on ingratitude. Surely our old Head would expire if he knew that in his school he harboured so many thankless Brutuses. Come, Clement, let us hear you recite the piece, and well.' 95

Clement stepped forward, shabby and barefoot, and with eyes downcast, began to recite the passage in a choked, monotonous tone. Now and again the schoolmaster threatened him with his rod, exhorting him to speak up. The boy would then raise his voice and quicken his words under the threat of the lash, but soon his voice sank back and the recitation resumed its muttered vein. 100

At last, however, the passage was finished. The acting Headmaster then spent some minutes more making the hapless boys the laughing-stock of their school friends. Only when he thought the school on the verge of becoming unmanageable did he dismiss the tormented boys with the words: 105

'Now go to your places. But bear in mind, every morning, until you show some appreciation for your resigning Headmaster, you shall come up here and stand in shame before the whole school.' 110

It was dusk, and the Dovecots were taking their one substantial meal of the day.

No one could think, looking at their home, that threepenny pieces, or even halfpennies, were to be had there for the asking. 115

The house was a poor, wretched coop of a room, through the black, water-stained shingles of which you could count a dozen blue glimpses of the sky. The walls of the shack were papered with old newspapers and magazines, discoloured with age and stained and spotted from roof to floor, torn in a score of places, to reveal the rotting, worm-eaten boards beneath. The small room was divided by a threadbare cotton screen depicting seagulls soaring up from a sea of faded blue. In the midst of this drab poverty the free, soaring seagulls, and the once gay pictures of the magazine pages were an unkind comment. 120 125

The Dovecots were a family of four: Dave and his wife Maud, Clement and his older sister Evelina.

Clement sat on the sanded floor of the poor sitting-room, his plate of rice between his legs; Evelina lolled over the one battered, depreciated mahogany table, picking at the coarse food with an adolescent discontent; Dave Dovecot, a grizzled, gangling[7] labourer, held his plate in his left hand, while with his right he piled his mouth from a peeling metal spoon; at the propped-open window of the room sat Mrs Dovecot, a long thread of a woman whose bones want had picked like an eagle. Her plate was resting on her lap, and she scraped and pecked and foraged her food like a scratching hen, while she took stock of the passers-by. 130 135

When Clement had finished, he took up his empty plate and, getting to his feet, went and stowed it away in the dark box of a kitchen. Returning, he slumped down beside his mother's chair and rested his head against her bony thigh. 140

7 **gangling** tall, thin

After a time he said:

'Ma, could I have the threepence I's been asking for Mr Megahey?'   145

'Hmn. Wa' threepence boy? Why in de name of de Lord must poor starving people got to find threepences for Jim Megahey what's got his belly sitting so pretty wi' fat?' parried Mrs Dovecot, though she knew well enough.

'I's told you and told you and told you, Ma. He's resigning and   150
we've all got to take threepence to give him,' explained Clement patiently once more.

'Hmn. Threepence is a lot o' money for us poor folk. Hmn. Go ax your father. See what *he* says.' Clement got to his feet reluctantly and moved slowly over to where his father was   155
sitting, for he knew from experience that, in parting with money, his father was a far harder nut to crack than his mother.

Dave Dovecot utilised the approach of his son by extending his empty plate. Clement took the plate to the kitchen. Then he turned once more to tackle his father.   160

'Can I have a threepence, Papa?' he shouted in his father's ear, for the old man was pretty nigh stone deaf.

'Eh-eh! What's that about a fence, Clement?'

This time Clement put his mouth completely into his father's ear and shouted until his dark face grew darker.   165

'Eh-eh! Don't shout at me,' was all he got for his pains. Don't you deafen me. What's that the young varmint says, Maud?'

Mrs Dovecot came over, and got him to understand after two or three attempts.

'Three pence, Maudie,' he cackled, 'three pence! Did yo' hear   170
thet, Maud? Did yo' ever hear the like? I'll bet you ain't never did. Three pence! The lad'll have money what I's got to sweat blood for, just to gi to thet Megahey what's got his bread so well buttered off 'pon both sides not to mention the middle. Three pence! Ha ha! ... Oh Maudie ...' And he broke down once   175
more in helpless laughter. Clements went out and sat under the breadfruit tree that grew before the door, resting his back against the trunk.

Evelina came to him there when the dusk was thick and sat beside him.   180

There was a close bond of understanding and companionship between these two. Clement leaned against her so that he could feel the warmth of her arms, warm as the still warm ground beneath him. Biting his nails he told her of his morning's shame.   185

She listened as attentively as a mother, and as she listened, she put her hand around his neck and drew his head gently down upon her young bosom.

When he had finished talking she put her lips down to his harsh curls, and thought for a long time. Then she said, with a little sigh: 190

'I know what we'll do, Clemmie. 'Member how 'fore I was took from school we big girls used to go out singing at Christmas? Well, we'll play waits. Only there'll be only you and me.'

Clement raised his head and gazed into her face in the starlight. 195

'Oh, Eve,' he said, 'but it ain't anyways near Christmas.'

'Never you mind,' she said. 'There's still some who'll give us a penny or two. You wait. I'll get our hats and then we'll be off.'

She got to her feet and slipped quickly into the house. She returned in a few moments carrying his cap in her hand, 200 her own hat of straw on her head. She settled his cap, then produced a comb.

'When we come to the shop we'll ask for a piece of bread paper,' she said, 'then you'll play the sax while I sing.'

They roamed far that night. Evelina's voice rose clear and true 205 to the accompaniment of the paper and comb, long after the moon came up and laid white hands upon the countryside.

At last Evelina said, jingling the coins which they had earned in the pockets of her dress:

'Let's make this our last and call it a day.' 210

The house with which they proposed to round off their tour had a pretentious[8] front of red brick. The greater part of the house was in darkness, but from the street the two could see a couple sitting in the open veranda[9].

Bravely, Evelina unlatched the street gate and lead the way 215 up the steps to the veranda.

'Good night, ' she greeted the pair in the shadows. 'We would like to sing for you.'

The woman chuckled softly and Evelina could see the white gleam of the man's teeth when he said, 'Sure.' 220

The children rendered their song. When they had finished the man got to his feet and approached them, delving in his pocket.

'Thanks for your singing,' he said kindly. 'It was very nice. May, give us some light for a moment.'

The woman got from her chair and leaning through a 225 window, pressed a light switch.

And as the light flooded the veranda little Clement was turned to stone, for the tall, greying man foraging the handful of coins was the retiring Headmaster, Mr Megahey.

Clement's scrambled retreat after Evelina had made her little 230 curtsy was perhaps unnecessary, since Mr Megahey had his glasses off and he didn't seem to recognise him.

8 **pretentious** showy

9 **veranda** porch with a roof

Out in the road, Evelina let out the laughter that had been welling inside her.

'Just think how we never thought of where your old Head 235
might've moved to after he left the Schoolmaster's house,'
she laughed. 'But he's gi'n us our biggest taking for the night,
anyway. He's gi'n us sixpence.'

They counted their takings in the middle of the white road in
the moonlight. When they had finished, Evelina poured the 240
coins back into her pocket and said:

'Now I going to tell you how we'll fix that brute, Mr Chase.'

On the following morning the acting Head, Mr Chase, kept his
word. Immediately after prayers the boys who had brought
no silver were lined up across the platform. They were but 245
eight of them this morning. Two had somehow managed
their threepenny pieces, while two or three others absented
themselves. Clement counted the line of boys as he took his
place among them.

As Mr Chase eyed their bowed heads in enjoyment, 250
Clement stepped forward, the eight pieces of silver upon his
extended palm.

'There are eight,' he told the gaping schoolmaster. 'One for
each of us.'

His voice struck through the silent school, clear and thrilling 255
as a star's light.

THE PIECES OF SILVER by Karl Sealy

The following Activities on this complete short story will develop further
your skills of analysing Prose texts. The questions asked here are the kind you
should ask yourself when reading Prose texts on your own. The Activities
suggest useful strategies for increasing your understanding of the story.

Activities 48 and 49 provide examples of the type of questions set on Prose
fiction texts.

43 Look at lines 1–15.

What are your first impressions of the school?

Write one paragraph, using brief quotations to support your answer.

44 Use separate sheets of paper to draw mind maps for the following:

- How Sealy presents the character of Clement
- How he presents the character of Mr Dovecot
- How he presents the character of Mrs Dovecot.

Collect information from relevant parts of the story.

On your mind maps write out brief, relevant quotations and comment on the effects of the key words.

45 Read the following lines again:

> *It was dusk, and the Dovecots were taking their one substantial meal of the day. No one could think, looking at their home, that threepenny pieces, or even halfpennies, were to be had there for the asking. The house was poor, wretched coop of a room, through the black, water-stained shingles of which you could count a dozen blue glimpses of the sky. The walls of the shack were papered with old newspapers and magazines, discoloured with age and stained and spotted from roof to floor, torn in a score of places, to reveal the rotting, worm-eaten boards beneath. The small room was divided by a threadbare cotton screen depicting seagulls soaring up from a sea of faded blue. In the midst of this drab poverty the free, soaring seagulls, and the once gay pictures of the magazine pages were an unkind comment.*

Write two paragraphs in which you explore how Sealy vividly brings to life the setting of the Dovecots' home.

Remember to use brief quotations and precise analytical comment in your answer.

46 Read lines 233–256:

How effective do you find the ending of the story? Think about:

- Evelina's words
- Mr Chase's reaction
- the description of Clement's voice.

Write one paragraph, quoting details from the story and commenting on the effects of key words and phrases.

47 Use a 'Quotation and Comment' table like the one shown below to record material for the following question:

In what ways does Sealy make Mr Chase such an unpleasant character?

Quotation	Comment
The stout, pompous, acting Headmaster	This initial description focuses immediately on Mr Chase's physical and personal qualities. The word 'pompous' suggests the narrator's disapproval of this self-important man.

You could use a list of bullet points or draw a mind map to plan your answer to the question in Activity 48. Do not spend more than 5 minutes on your plan.

48 Using the information from Activity 47, write a critical response to the following question:

In what ways does Sealy make Mr Chase such an unpleasant character?

Spend 45 minutes on this question.

49 Write a response to the following empathic question:

You are Clement at the end of the story, after giving Mr Chase eight pieces of silver. Write your thoughts.

Spend 45 minutes on this question.

Extension

In groups of four, act out the scene in the Dovecot household (lines 128–178). Do not worry about props. Focus on the following:

- the position and movements of the characters
- the lines they speak.

Use a copy of the scene to indicate the lines spoken by:

- Clement
- Evelina
- Dave Dovecot
- Mrs Dovecot

Tip

For your examination Prose set text, you should have your own notes on the areas in this checklist.

Quick recap
Developing an informed personal response

Different readers engage with Prose texts in different ways. If you adopt a disciplined approach to study, you will be able to develop a convincing personal response to the fiction you read. The following is a checklist that helps you to appreciate the detail of Prose texts: both the content and the ways in which the content is presented.

How does the writer do the following?

- Begin the text
- Develop the plot
- Present the main themes (or deeper meanings)
- Introduce and develop characters
- Establish setting(s)
- Convey mood and shifts in mood
- Use first or third person narration
- Sequence and organise events
- End the story.

 **Further reading**

Choose three of the books from the list below unless they happen to be a set text you are already studying. Then do some research in a library or on the internet to find out what each of these books is about. Next, select one that you think you would most like to read. You may not have time to read the whole book, so read one or two chapters from it. Don't forget to return to the book once your exams are over!

Pride and Prejudice by Jane Austen
Jane Eyre by Charlotte Brontë
Brave New World by Aldous Huxley
Animal Farm by George Orwell
Of Mice and Men by John Steinbeck
Things Fall Apart by Chinua Achebe
Lord of the Flies by William Golding
When Rain Clouds Gather by Bessie Head
The Prime of Miss Jean Brodie by Muriel Spark
I'm the King of the Castle by Susan Hill
Fasting, Feasting by Anita Desai
The Good Earth by Pearl S. Buck

Unit summary

In this Unit you have built on the skills of close reading developed in Unit 3: 'Responding to Poetry'. You have used active learning skills such as highlighting, annotation, lists, tables and mind maps. You have learned about the need to explore both the content of Prose texts and the techniques writers use to present characters and themes, as well as to establish setting and mood.

As with Poetry, you have learned how important it is to comment in critical essays on the effects of writers' use of language and structure. You should never be satisfied with simply *identifying* devices. For example, you need to explore *how* writers use first person narration and not simply say that they do. The Activities have been designed to help you develop your own independent responses to the ways in which Prose writers write.

You have learned to identify with a given character and to write in a suitable voice for that character, when answering empathic questions.

You have learned that you must always support your personal response by referring to the detail of texts. The next Unit will reinforce these skills as you consider extracts from the third main literary form – Drama.

UNIT 5 Responding to Drama

Objectives
In this Unit, you will:

- read closely a number of extracts from plays

- develop skills you need for responding sensitively to the meanings of plays

- analyse the ways dramatists use form, structure and language to create and shape meanings

- use appropriate terminology when responding to Drama texts

- gain confidence in giving informed personal responses to Drama texts.

Writers of plays are referred to as **dramatists**. Another commonly used term is 'playwright'.

The following paragraphs will help you to understand the objectives of this Unit in more detail, and explain how each section of the Unit will develop the knowledge and skills you need when reading and responding to Drama.

Read closely a number of extracts from plays

In this unit you will work through a number of extracts from plays by Shakespeare and other **dramatists**.

You will need to provide a detailed response to a Drama text in your Set Texts Paper 1 or 4. You may also need to engage with Drama in one of the following:

- Set Text (Paper 5)
- Coursework.

There is no Drama text on the Unseen Paper (Paper 3).

Respond sensitively to the meanings of plays

Plays are intended for performance on a stage in front of an audience. This means that we read plays differently from the way we read poems and prose fiction. Plays have their own distinctive appearance when set out on the page of a book – as you will see.

Because plays are written for performance, it is important that you practise reading the lines spoken by characters. Some of the Activities in this Unit will also help you to consider how particular scenes might be staged.

The skills covered in this Unit build on the close reading skills you practised in Units 3 and 4 on responding to Poetry and Prose. As in those Units, some unusual or difficult words will be explained for you. You may, however, need to refer to a dictionary for other words you are not familiar with. Remember that it is your responsibility as an active learner to find out the meanings of words. This stage of your learning cannot be skipped as you work towards a detailed appreciation of the play. After all, you will not read characters' lines effectively if you do not understand the words they say.

You already appreciate that active learners write as well as read. In studying Drama texts, you should use note-making strategies introduced in earlier Units:

- Annotating copies of key scenes
- Making lists
- Recording your information in tables
- Creating mind maps.

Analyse the ways dramatists use form, structure and language

In the previous Units on responding to Poetry and Prose, you considered *how* writers write as well as *what* they write. You looked at the ways they use form, structure and language to convey their meanings. In Drama texts, too, it is important to consider the *ways* in which dramatists write as well as the content of their plays.

In Units 3 and 4 you learned how to analyse closely writers' use of language and structure. This remains a key area of study for plays too, but in responding to a dramatist's use of form a different approach is required.

Whilst poems and Prose fiction are intended for reading, plays are intended for performance on a stage. This fact influences the way we 'read' plays. In the theatre the words on the page are brought to life. A large number of people have a role in creating this theatrical experience for the audience. Actors and directors will bring their own **interpretation** of how the dialogue on the page should sound in **performance**. Decisions will be made about how the settings of the play should appear on stage: lighting, sound, music and **props** contribute to the overall performance.

It is important to remember all of this as you read a play. For every scene in your set text play, for example, it is important that you do the following:

- Visualise how it might appear on stage
- Visualise how certain actions by characters might be performed
- Consider the different ways lines might be spoken by actors.

Tip

There are two key differences between plays and novels:

- Plays are intended as shared experiences in a theatre whereas novels are for personal reading
- Plays might last two hours or more whilst a long novel can take days to read.

Key term

Interpretation is how directors and actors offer a particular 'reading' of how characters' lines might be spoken or actions performed on the stage.

Performance of a play brings to life the words on the page for an audience in a theatre.

Props (short for 'properties') are items used in plays, such as the bloody dagger in the extract from *Macbeth* on page 114.

Link

Dialogue was a word you were introduced to in Unit 4 on responding to Prose texts. It refers to the words characters speak. In prose fiction, dialogue is usually set out within speech marks. In drama texts, the words spoken follow a character's name: see any of the extracts in this Unit.

Some of the key areas for study you will consider are the ways in which dramatists do the following:

* Begin plays
* Present characters
* Explore themes
* Create settings and mood
* Use language
* Use structure.

You need to show that you can evaluate the choices dramatists make and the effects they create. They make deliberate decisions about the words they use and the ways in which they organise their content. They think carefully about their use of structure in the following ways:

* Structure within a speech by one character
* Structure in extended dialogue between characters
* Structure within a scene
* Structure within the whole play.

Use appropriate terminology when responding to Drama texts

Many of the terms introduced in Unit 3 'Responding to Poetry' are also relevant for Drama texts. Characters in drama will use metaphors and other forms of speech – just as we do in daily life. Already in this Unit, you have come across words such as dramatist, performance and props. As you read on, you will encounter other terms which relate specifically to Drama texts.

You know that using literary terms is never enough. Your job is not merely to identify or describe literary devices used by writers. Analysis is a higher order skill than mere description: you have to consider the *effects* of words chosen by the writers.

Gain confidence in giving informed personal responses to Drama texts

Link

In Unit 6, 'Developing effective writing skills', you will explore in detail how to write successful critical and empathic responses to texts. You will also find guidance on what examiners will give you credit for in your written responses.

In examinations or Coursework responses to Drama texts, you have to present your point of view convincingly in order to persuade your reader of the merits of your argument. This Unit builds on the work of previous Units. In critical responses to Drama, you need to:

* support your points by detailed references to the play
* analyse closely the effects of particular words
* analyse closely the effects of particular actions.

As with Prose texts, you have the option of answering an empathic question on Drama set texts. In these questions, you are asked to assume the voice of a particular character at a specific moment in the play.

Empathic questions can help you to appreciate the detail of plays you study. This is because you have to think very carefully about events in the play from the viewpoint of one particular character.

As you work through this Unit, you should read the extracts and then do the Activities that follow them.

Responding to characters and themes

From THE GLASS MENAGERIE by Tennessee Williams

A stage performance showing Tom with sister Laura (left) and mother Amanda (right).

[LEGEND ON SCREEN: 'YOU THINK I'M IN LOVE WITH CONTINENTAL SHOEMAKERS?']

[*Before the stage is lighted, the violent voices of* TOM *and* AMANDA *are heard.*

They are quarrelling behind the portières. In front of them stands LAURA *with clenched hands and panicky expression.*   5

A clear pool of light on her figure throughout this scene.]

TOM	What in Christ's name am I –
AMANDA	[*shrilly*] Don't you use that –
TOM	Supposed to do!
AMANDA	Expression! Not in my –
TOM	Ohhh!

10

AMANDA   Presence! Have you gone out of your senses?

TOM   I have, that's true, *driven* out!

AMANDA   What is the matter with you, you – big – big IDIOT!

TOM   Look! – I've got *no thing*, no single thing –   15

AMANDA   Lower your voice!

TOM   In my life here that I can call my OWN! Everything is –

AMANDA   Stop that shouting!

TOM   Yesterday you confiscated my books! You had the nerve to –   20

AMANDA   I took that horrible novel back to the library – yes! That hideous book by that insane Mr Lawrence[1]. [TOM *laughs wildly.*] I cannot control the output of diseased minds or people who cater to them – [TOM *laughs still more wildly.*] BUT I WON'T ALLOW SUCH FILTH   25 BROUGHT INTO MY HOUSE! No, no, no, no, no!

TOM   House, house! Who pays the rent on it, who makes a slave of himself to –

AMANDA   [*fairly screeching*] Don't you D A R E to –

TOM   No, no, *I* mustn't say things! *I've* got to just –   30

AMANDA   Let me tell you –

TOM   I don't want to hear any more! [*He tears the portières open. The upstage area is lit with a turgid smoky red glow.*]

[AMANDA'S *hair is in metal curlers and she wears a very old bathrobe, much*   35 *too large for her slight figure, a relic of the faithless Mr Wingfield. An upright typewriter and a wild disarray of manuscripts are on the drop-leaf table. The quarrel was probably precipitated by* AMANDA'S *interruption of his creative labour. A chair lying overthrown on the floor.*

Their gesticulating shadows are cast on the ceiling by the fiery glow.]   40

AMANDA   You *will* hear more, you –

TOM   No, I won't hear more, I'm going out!

AMANDA   You come right back in –

TOM   Out, out, out! Because I'm –

AMANDA   Come back here, Tom Wingfield! I'm not through   45 talking to you!

TOM   Oh, go –

LAURA   [*desperately*] – Tom!

1 **Mr Lawrence** D. H. Lawrence, English novelist 1885–1930

AMANDA   You're going to listen, and no more insolence from you! I'm at the end of my patience!   50

[*He comes back toward her.*]

TOM   What do you think I'm at? Aren't I supposed to have any patience to reach the end of, Mother? I know, I know. It seems unimportant to you, what I'm *doing* – what I *want* to do – having a little *difference* between them! You don't think that –   55

AMANDA   I think you've been doing things that you're ashamed of. That's why you act like this. I don't believe that you go every night to the movies. Nobody goes to the movies night after night. Nobody in their right mind goes to the movies as often as you pretend to. People don't go to the movies at nearly midnight, and movies don't let out at two a.m. Come in stumbling. Muttering to yourself like a maniac! You get three hours' sleep and then go to work. Oh, I can picture the way you're doing down there. Moping, doping, because you're in no condition.   60   65

TOM   [*wildly*] No, I'm in no condition!

2 **jeopardize** put at risk

AMANDA   What right have you got to jeopardize[2] your job? Jeopardize the security of us all? How do you think we'd manage if you were –   70

TOM   Listen! You think I'm crazy about the *warehouse*? [*He bends fiercely toward her slight figure.*] You think I'm in love with the Continental Shoemakers? You think I want to spend fifty-five *years* down there in that – *celotex interior*! with – *fluorescent* – *tubes*! Look! I'd rather somebody picked up a crowbar and battered out my brains – than go back mornings! I *go*! Every time you come in yelling that God damn *'Rise and Shine!' 'Rise and Shine!'* I say myself, 'How *lucky dead* people are! 'But I get up. I *go*! For sixty-five dollars a month I give up all that I dream of doing and being *ever*! And you say self – *self*s' all I ever think of. Why, listen, if self is what I thought of, Mother, I'd be where he is – GONE! [*Pointing to father's picture.*] As far as the system of transportation reaches! [*He starts past her. She grabs his arm.*] Don't grab at me, Mother!   75   80   85

AMANDA   Where are you going?

TOM   I'm going to the *movies*!

AMANDA   I don't believe that lie!

Key term

Stage directions provide information to directors, actors and others involved in bringing the script to life on the stage. In this scene the lighting technicians are directed (on line 6) to keep a 'clear pool of light' on Laura, a character who is virtually silent throughout the extract. In this way the lighting gives importance to a character who has to speak only one word.

Tip

When referring to stage directions, you should remember that these cannot be read by the audience when watching the play. You should not comment on the way the stage directions are written. You should comment on what they reveal about the characters' actions or feelings.

Exploring the extract from THE GLASS MENAGERIE by Tennessee Williams

This extract from a 1944 American play provides a good introduction to the features of a Drama script. The main focus on stage is an argument between the mother, Amanda, and her son, Tom. A third character, the daughter Laura, speaks once, but has 'a clear pool of light on her figure' throughout the extract.

The **stage directions**, in italics, are given within brackets. This sets them clearly apart from the words to be spoken by the actors. It is one of the distinctive features of Drama texts.

Reading stage directions will help you to visualise how the play might appear on stage as you read through it on your own or in class.

1 Read the stage directions in this extract carefully. They serve a number of different purposes. Match the following list of purposes to the stage directions in the table below. Record your answers in a table like this, using each purpose *once* only.

The purpose of stage directions is to give information about the following:

- Volume of the characters' voices
- What the character looks like
- How the character behaves
- Lighting
- Appearance of the set.

Stage direction	Purpose (what does the stage direction tell us about?)
… *the violent voices of TOM and AMANDA are heard. They are quarrelling* …	Volume of the characters' voices and the intensity of their feelings
AMANDA'S hair is in metal curlers and she wears a very old bathrobe, much too large for her slight figure …	
A clear pool of light on her figure throughout this scene.	
An upright typewriter and a wild disarray of manuscripts are on the drop-leaf table.	
… *with clenched hands and panicky expression.*	

This Activity shows you just some of the ways in which stage directions can be used in plays. They are helpful in creating a picture of what a particular scene might look like on stage. They also provide guidance about how words should be spoken and, in so doing, set the mood for the scene.

2 Williams uses stage directions to convey other information about characters. Write down concisely what you think the following pieces of information reveal about the characters in this extract.

a Amanda's bathrobe is described as '*a relic of the faithless Mr Wingfield*'.
b *The quarrel was probably precipitated by AMANDA'S interruption of his creative labour.*

Find a space in which you can act out the extract. Do not try to recreate the set with props. Concentrate instead on how you think the characters should speak and move.

3 In small groups, read through the extract once.

Then discuss how the following characters might speak their lines:

- Amanda
- Tom.

Take into account the following:

- What Williams says in the stage directions
- The words the characters actually speak
- The spoken words which are capitalised or in italics.

4 This extract portrays **conflict** between mother and son.

Write a paragraph, of about 150 words, in which you summarise what they are arguing about.

5 List the impressions you have of Amanda as you read the following lines in the table below. Use a copy of the table to record your impressions.

Lines spoken by Amanda	Your impressions of Amanda
Don't use that – *Expression! Not in my –*	
Lower your voice!	The way Amanda issues commands here makes it sound as if she is addressing a naughty boy rather than her grown-up son.
I took that horrible novel back to the library – yes!	
BUT I WON'T ALLOW SUCH FILTH BROUGHT INTO MY HOUSE! No, no, no, no, no!	

Key term

Dramatic **conflict** between characters can often be found at the heart of plays. Such conflict helps to create tension and make a scene such as this particularly dramatic. This engages the attention of the audience.

Tip

In plays, writers present characters mainly through what they say. By contrast, Prose fiction writers have much greater flexibility. This is because Prose writers can describe the thoughts and feelings of characters, as well as telling us what they say.

Lines spoken by Amanda	Your impressions of Amanda
People don't go to the movies at nearly midnight, and movies don't let out at two a.m. Come in stumbling. Muttering to yourself like a maniac!	
Jeopardize the security of us all?	

In plays, writers present characters largely through what they say and also from what other characters say about them. As you can see from this extract, stage directions can also contribute to our appreciation of characters. Prose fiction writers have greater flexibility, as they can show readers what characters are thinking.

6 Tom is clearly frustrated with his mother and with his life in general. One of the themes in the play is how trapped Tom feels both at home and at work. He feels unable to be himself and live the life he wants. He lacks independence.

▶ Select five lines from the extract which best illustrate this theme. Comment fully on the effects of your chosen lines. Use a table like this to record your answer. Two examples are given for you.

Tom's line	Comment on effect
I've got no thing, no single thing … In my life here that I can call my OWN!	This gives a powerful impression of how oppressive Tom feels life at home is. It seems that he is not allowed to have his own possessions. His mother even confiscates his books. Tom lacks space in which he can be himself.
Yesterday you confiscated my books! You had the nerve to –	

7 This Activity asks you to empathise with Tom.

You are Tom later that day, thinking about the row that had taken place earlier.

Write your thoughts in a diary entry for that day. Write about 250 words.

Remember to:

- stay faithful to the original text
- capture the thoughts that Tom is likely to have, based on the evidence of the extract
- use a voice that is recognisably Tom's voice.

Extension

A useful Activity for getting to grips with the detail of plays is hot-seating. In this small-group Activity, one person should take the role of Tom whilst others in the group fire questions at him. The student playing the role of Tom should answer the questions using evidence in the extract. Here are some useful starter questions:

- Why are you so angry with your mother?
- What do you hate about your life at home?
- What do you hate about your work?

From DEATH OF A SALESMAN
by Arthur Miller

In this photograph from a stage production of *Death of a Salesman*, the actor on the left is playing Happy and the one on the right is Biff. How does this photograph add to your appreciation of these two characters?

BIFF   I tell ya, Hap, I don't know what the future is. I don't know – what I'm supposed to want.

HAPPY   What do you mean?

BIFF   Well, I spent six or seven years after high school trying to work myself up. Shipping clerk, salesman, business   5 of one kind or another. And it's a measly manner of existence. To get on that subway on the hot mornings in summer. To devote your whole life to keeping stock, or making phone calls, or selling or buying. To suffer fifty weeks of the year for the sake of a two-week vacation,   10 when all you really desire is to be outdoors, with your shirt off. And always to have to get ahead of the next fella. And still – that's how you build a future.

HAPPY   Well, you really enjoy it on a farm? Are you content out there?   15

BIFF   [*with rising agitation*] Hap, I've had twenty or thirty different kinds of job since I left home before the war, and it always turns out the same. I just realized it lately. In Nebraska when I herded cattle, and the Dakotas, and Arizona, and now in Texas. It's why I came home now, I guess, because I realized it. This farm I work on, it's spring there now, see? And they've got about fifteen new colts. There's nothing more inspiring or – beautiful than the sight of a mare and a new colt. And it's cool there now, see? Texas is cool now, and it's spring. And whenever spring comes to where I am, I suddenly get the feeling, my God, I'm not gettin' anywhere. What the hell am I doing, playing around with horses, twenty-eight dollars a week! I'm thirty-four years old, I oughta be makin' my future. That's when I come running home. And now, I get here, and I don't know what to do with myself. [*After a pause*] I've always made a point of not wasting my life, and everytime I come back here I know that all I've done is to waste my life.   20   25   30

HAPPY   You're a poet, you know that, Biff? You're a – you're an idealist!   35

BIFF   No, I'm mixed up very bad. Maybe I oughta get married. Maybe I oughta get stuck into something. Maybe that's my trouble. I'm like a boy. I'm not married, I'm not in business, I just – I'm like a boy. Are you content, Hap? You're a success, aren't you? Are you content?   40

HAPPY   Hell, no!

BIFF   Why? You're making money, aren't you?

HAPPY   [*moving about with energy, expressiveness*] All I can do now is wait for the merchandise manager to die. And suppose I get to be merchandise manager? He's a good friend of mine, and he just built a terrific estate[1] on Long Island[2]. And he lived there about two months and sold it, and now he's building another one. He can't enjoy it once it's finished. And I know that's just what I would do. I don't know what the hell I'm workin' for. Sometimes I sit in my apartment – all alone. And I think of the rent I'm paying. And it's crazy. But then, it's what I always wanted. My own apartment, a car, and plenty of women. And still, goddammit, I'm lonely.   45   50   55

BIFF   [*with enthusiasm*] Listen, why don't you come out West with me?

1 **estate** property

2 **Long Island** island in southeastern New York

HAPPY   You and I, heh?

BIFF   Sure, maybe we could buy a ranch. Raise cattle, use our
muscles. Men built like we are should be working out   60
in the open.

HAPPY   [*avidly*] The Loman Brothers, heh?

BIFF   [*with vast affection*] Sure, we'd be known all over the
counties!

HAPPY   [*enthralled*] That's what I dream about, Biff. Sometimes   65
I want to just rip my clothes off in the middle of the
store and outbox that goddam merchandise manager.
I mean I can outbox, outrun, and outlift anybody in that
store, and I have to take orders from those common,
petty sons-of-bitches till I can't stand it any more.   70

BIFF   I'm tellin' you, kid, if you were with me I'd be happy
out there.

Exploring the extract from DEATH OF A SALESMAN by Arthur Miller

The extract from *The Glass Menagerie* portrayed an intense conflict between
mother and grown-up son. This extract presents a quieter extended
dialogue between two brothers: Biff Loman and his younger brother,
Happy. It is from Arthur Miller's 1949 play *Death of a Salesman*.

In this dialogue the characters reveal a lot about themselves to each other
and, of course, to the audience. If the audience is to engage with the
characters, they need to be convincing. In this extract, the dialogue explores
how the characters are in different ways dissatisfied with their lives.

8 With a partner, read the extract aloud.

Then discuss ways in which you might improve your performance.
Think about the following:

- Which lines do you find particularly sad?
- Which lines do you think are more hopeful or optimistic?
- Which lines do you think reveal most about each character?
- How do the brief stage directions help your performance?

Next, read the extract aloud as if you were on the stage. As you read,
think carefully about:

- words requiring emphasis
- changes in your tone of voice
- the **pace** of your reading
- pauses for dramatic effect.

Tip

When writing about plays,
remember to write about
effects on the *audience*
rather than the *reader*. This
shows the examiner that
you understand you are
writing about a play, and not
Prose fiction.

Key term

Pace refers to how fast
or how slowly you read a
particular line. It can also
refer to the speed at which
one line follows another.

Tip

It is worth spending some
time deciding how lines
might be read. This helps
you to identify more
closely with:

- the character's feelings
- their motivation for acting
  or behaving as they do.

9 Look at lines 1–40 – up to Biff's line '... I'm like a boy'.

Use evidence from the extract to answer the following questions about the way Miller presents the character of Biff. Write a paragraph of about 100 words for each question.

a What past life or **back story** does Miller provide for Biff?

b In what ways does Miller present Biff's dissatisfaction with life at the age of thirty-four?

10 Look at lines 40–72, from Biff's line 'Are you content, Hap?' to the end of the extract.

Draw a mind map which illustrates the way Miller presents the character of Happy in this scene. Start with the words 'Presentation of Happy' in the middle of the mind map, as in the example below. This will help you to explore in greater detail the relevant material in the extract.

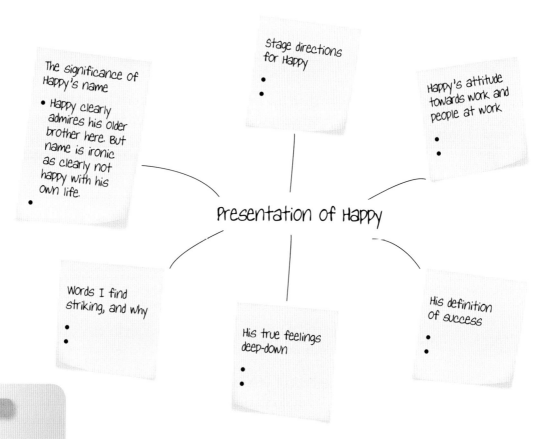

11 In this Activity you are asked to consider how Miller *vividly* conveys both Biff and Happy's dissatisfaction with their lives. How does Miller bring their dissatisfaction powerfully to life on the stage? Consider the following question:

How does Miller vividly convey the characters' dissatisfaction with their lives?

Activities 8–10 have in different ways prepared you to answer this question. Write your response in two paragraphs.

Remember to use brief quotations to support your points. And comment precisely on the effects created by the words Miller gives his characters. Here is an example of how to link quotation and comment:

Biff's opening remark 'I don't know – what I'm supposed to want' shows that he feels his life is without direction. His dismissal of his life working in business as 'a measly manner of existence' suggests that he wants more from life ...

Link

In the extract from *The Glass Menagerie* Tom is unhappy working in the warehouse. Tom, Biff and Happy are all in different ways resentful of the kind of work found in cities.

Both Williams and Miller present in dramatic form the conflict between the real-life world of work and the inner dreams the characters have of a happier life. In plays such major themes are communicated through the words the characters speak.

 In the extract Miller uses the dialogue between the brothers to explore an important theme: how work affects people's feelings about who they are.

On a copy of the extract, highlight words and phrases which show:

- Biff's thoughts about working in the city
- Biff's thoughts about working on a farm
- Happy's attitude towards his work.

Then use a mind map to illustrate how Miller presents the contrasts between working on a farm and working in business.

This Activity will help you to map out clearly the differences between two types of work, and attitudes towards work.

Quick recap
Responding to characters and themes

As you study characters and themes in plays, consider the following questions.

Aspects of characterisation
- What do stage directions reveal about the character's appearance?
- What do stage directions tell you about the character's personal qualities?
- What impression do you form of the character from *what* they say and *how* they speak?
- What impression do you form of the character from how they behave?
- In what ways does the character contrast with other characters?
- Is there a conflict between the character and other characters?
- Is there a conflict within the character?

Aspects of themes

- What do characters have to say about the big issues in life?
- How are characters used to illustrate different aspects of themes?

Active learning strategies

Use one or more of these strategies to improve your appreciation of the way characters and themes are presented in plays.

- Highlight and annotate key words
- List points
- Use 'Quotation and Comment' tables
- Write a summary
- Draw mind maps
- Write notes from the character's viewpoint.

Responding to structure and language

From A TASTE OF HONEY
by Shelagh Delaney

What does this image from the 1961 film of *A Taste of Honey* reveal about the characters of mother and daughter?

SCENE ONE

The stage represents a comfortless flat in Manchester and the street outside. Jazz music. Enter HELEN ... and her daughter, JO. They are loaded with baggage.

HELEN   Well! This is the place.

JO   And I don't like it.   5

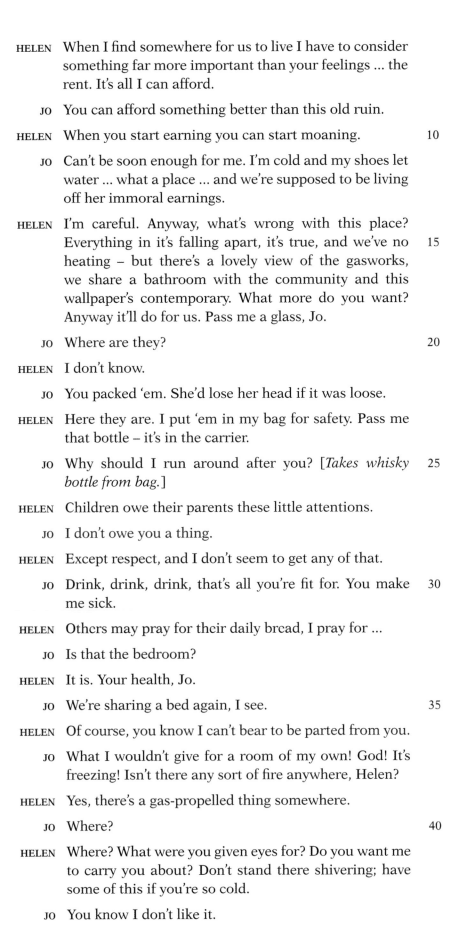

HELEN   When I find somewhere for us to live I have to consider something far more important than your feelings ... the rent. It's all I can afford.

JO   You can afford something better than this old ruin.

HELEN   When you start earning you can start moaning.   10

JO   Can't be soon enough for me. I'm cold and my shoes let water ... what a place ... and we're supposed to be living off her immoral earnings.

HELEN   I'm careful. Anyway, what's wrong with this place? Everything in it's falling apart, it's true, and we've no   15 heating – but there's a lovely view of the gasworks, we share a bathroom with the community and this wallpaper's contemporary. What more do you want? Anyway it'll do for us. Pass me a glass, Jo.

JO   Where are they?   20

HELEN   I don't know.

JO   You packed 'em. She'd lose her head if it was loose.

HELEN   Here they are. I put 'em in my bag for safety. Pass me that bottle – it's in the carrier.

JO   Why should I run around after you? [*Takes whisky*   25 *bottle from bag.*]

HELEN   Children owe their parents these little attentions.

JO   I don't owe you a thing.

HELEN   Except respect, and I don't seem to get any of that.

JO   Drink, drink, drink, that's all you're fit for. You make   30 me sick.

HELEN   Others may pray for their daily bread, I pray for ...

JO   Is that the bedroom?

HELEN   It is. Your health, Jo.

JO   We're sharing a bed again, I see.   35

HELEN   Of course, you know I can't bear to be parted from you.

JO   What I wouldn't give for a room of my own! God! It's freezing! Isn't there any sort of fire anywhere, Helen?

HELEN   Yes, there's a gas-propelled thing somewhere.

JO   Where?   40

HELEN   Where? What were you given eyes for? Do you want me to carry you about? Don't stand there shivering; have some of this if you're so cold.

JO   You know I don't like it.

| HELEN | Have you tried it? | 45 |

| JO | No. |

| HELEN | Then get it down you! [*She wanders around the room searching for fire.*] "Where!" she says. She can never see anything till she falls over it. Now, where's it got to? I know I saw it here somewhere . . . one of those shilling in the slot affairs; the landlady pointed it out to me as part of the furniture and fittings. I don't know. Oh! It'll turn up. What's up with you now? | 50 |

| JO | I don't like the smell of it. |

| HELEN | You don't smell it, you drink it! It consoles you. | 55 |

| JO | What do you need consoling about? |

| HELEN | Life! Come on, give it to me if you've done with it. I'll soon put it in a safe place. [*Drinks.*] |

| JO | You're knocking it back worse than ever. |

| HELEN | Oh! Well, it's one way of passing time while I'm waiting for something to turn up. And it usually does if I drink hard enough. Oh my God! I've caught a shocking cold from somebody. Have you got a clean hanky, Jo? Mine's wringing wet with dabbing at my nose all day. | 60 |

| JO | Have this, it's nearly clean. Isn't that light awful? I do hate to see an unshaded electric light bulb dangling from the ceiling like that. | 65 |

| HELEN | Well, don't look at it then. |

| JO | Can I have a chair, Helen? I'll put my scarf round it. [JO *takes chair from* HELEN, *stands on it and wraps her scarf round light bulb – burning herself in the process.*] | 70 |

| HELEN | Wouldn't she get on your nerves? Just when I was going to take the weight off my feet for five minutes. Oh! My poor old nose. |

| JO | Christ! It's hot. | 75 |

| HELEN | Why can't you leave things alone? Oh! she gets me down. I'll buy a proper shade tomorrow. It's running like a tap. This is the third hanky today. |

| JO | Tomorrow? What makes you think we're going to live that long? The roof's leaking! | 80 |

| HELEN | Is it? No, it's not, it's just condensation. |

| JO | Was it raining when you took the place? |

| HELEN | It is a bit of a mess, isn't it. |

JO   You always have to rush off into things. You never think.   85

HELEN   Oh well, we can always find something else.

JO   But what are you looking for? Every place we find is the same.

HELEN   Oh! Every time I turn my head my eyeballs hurt. Can't we have a bit of peace for five minutes?   90

JO   I'll make some coffee.

HELEN   Do what you like. I feel rotten. I've no business being out of bed.

Exploring the extract from A TASTE OF HONEY by Shelagh Delaney

This extract is the opening to Shelagh Delaney's 1958 play *A Taste of Honey*. The opening stage direction sets the scene and helps us to visualise what is happening on stage.

The opening of a play has to work hard to engage the audience's attention right away. Here, Helen and her daughter, Jo, enter the stage loaded with baggage. The immediate conflict between the two characters contributes to the dramatic impact.

 **Tip**

Within the overall structure of a play, the opening is very important. It has to:

- set the scene
- introduce characters
- engage the interest of the audience about what happens next.

13 Read the extract carefully.

From the stage directions and from the words spoken what picture do you form of the setting?

Using bullets, list your points in the order they occur in the extract. Start with:

- It is set in a 'comfortless' flat, which the daughter describes as 'an old ruin'.
- There's no heating.

14 Read the extract aloud with a partner. Discuss the most effective ways of speaking your character's lines. Aim for a polished performance.

15 On a copy of the extract, highlight those lines spoken by Helen which you think convey her character most strikingly. Then use annotation to explain what the lines reveal about her character. For example:

Jo's views not as important to Helen as financial considerations

I have to consider something far more important than your feelings … the rent.

16 Using a 'Quotation and Comment' table like the one below, select the evidence you could use to answer the following question:

How does Delaney encourage you to feel sympathy for Jo as you read this extract?

Quotation	Comment
Helen: When you start earning you can start moaning.	Right from the start of the play Delaney portrays Jo's mother as lacking affection towards her daughter. Jo's views are not important and will not be listened to until she makes a contribution to the rent.

17 Attempt the following empathic task:

You are Jo, looking back on your first day in the flat.
Write your thoughts.

Activities 13–16 have helped you to consider the detail of the extract.

In your response to the question, make sure you:

- write about 250 words
- create and sustain a convincing voice for Jo's thoughts
- set your answer clearly in the world of the play.

18 Working in pairs, read each other's response to Activity 17.

Note down any words or expressions that you think Jo would *not* use.

Discuss ways in which the responses might be improved.

 **Extension**

With your partner, rehearse for a performance of this extract. Consider carefully:

- emphasis of particular words
- the changing tone of voice of the characters
- the pace of delivering the lines
- use of dramatic pauses.

From MACBETH (Act 2, Scene 2)
by William Shakespeare

What impact do you think the sight of the blood on Macbeth's hands would have on an audience?

MACBETH   I have done the deed. Didst thou not hear a noise?

LADY MACBETH   I heard the owl scream and the crickets cry.   15
Did not you speak?

MACBETH   When?

LADY MACBETH   Now.

MACBETH   As I descended?

LADY MACBETH   Ay.   20

MACBETH   Hark, who lies i'th' second chamber?

LADY MACBETH   Donaldbain[1].

MACBETH   This is a sorry sight.

LADY MACBETH   A foolish thought, to say a sorry sight.

MACBETH   There's one did laugh in's sleep, and one cried,
'Murder!',   25
That they did wake each other; I stood, and
heard them,
But they did say their prayers, and addressed
them
Again to sleep.

LADY MACBETH   There are two lodged together.

1 **Donaldbain** a son of the murdered
King Duncan

MACBETH	One cried 'God bless us!' and 'Amen' the other,
	As they had seen me with these hangman's hands. 30
	List'ning their fear, I could not say 'Amen'
	When they did say 'God bless us.'
LADY MACBETH	Consider it not so deeply.
MACBETH	But wherefore could not I pronounce 'Amen'?
	I had most need of blessing, and 'Amen' 35
	Stuck in my throat.
LADY MACBETH	These deeds must not be thought
	After these ways; so, it will make us mad.

2 **Methought** I thought

3 **ravelled** untangled

4 **Balm of** medicine for

MACBETH	Methought[2] I heard a voice cry, 'Sleep no more:
	Macbeth does murder sleep', the innocent sleep,
	Sleep that knits up the ravelled[3] sleeve of care, 40
	The death of each day's life, sore labour's bath,
	Balm of[4] hurt minds, great nature's second course,
	Chief nourisher in life's feast.
LADY MACBETH	What do you mean?
MACBETH	Still it cried, 'Sleep no more' to all the house;
	'Glamis hath murdered sleep, and therefore
	Cawdor 45
	Shall sleep no more: Macbeth shall sleep no more.'

LADY MACBETH	Who was it, that thus cried? Why, worthy thane,
	You do unbend your noble strength to think
	So brain-sickly of things. Go get some water

5 **witness** evidence

	And wash this filthy witness[5] from your hand. 50
	Why did you bring these daggers from the place?
	They must lie there. Go carry them and smear

6 **grooms** guards

	The sleepy grooms[6] with blood.
MACBETH	I'll go no more.
	I am afraid to think what I have done;
	Look on't again I dare not.
LADY MACBETH	Infirm of purpose! 55
	Give me the daggers. The sleeping and the dead
	Are but as pictures; 'tis the eye of childhood
	That fears a painted devil. If he do bleed,

7 **gild** smear

	I'll gild[7] the faces of the grooms withal,
	For it must seem their guilt.
	[*Exit*]

[*Knock within*]

MACBETH	Whence is that knocking? 60
	How is't with me, when every noise appals me?

8 **Neptune** god of the sea (in Roman mythology)

9 **multitudinous** many

10 **incarnadine** make blood-red

What hands are here? Ha: they pluck out mine eyes.
Will all great Neptune's[8] ocean wash this blood
Clean from my hand? No: this my hand will rather
The multitudinous[9] seas incarnadine[10],   65
Making the green one red.

[*Enter* LADY MACBETH]

LADY MACBETH My hands are of your colour, but I shame
To wear a heart so white.

[*Knock within*]

               I hear a knocking
At the south entry. Retire we to our chamber;
A little water clears us of this deed.   70
How easy is it, then! Your constancy
Hath left you unattended.

[*Knock within*]

               Hark, more knocking.
Get on your night-gown, lest occasion call us,
And show us to be watchers. Be not lost
So poorly in your thoughts.   75

MACBETH To know my deed, 'twere best not know my self.

[*Knock within*]

Wake Duncan with thy knocking: I would thou
   couldst.

[*Exeunt*]

Exploring the extract from MACBETH by William Shakespeare

The extract from Macbeth comes at a key moment in the play, just after Macbeth has murdered King Duncan. The murder takes place offstage. The horror of it is conveyed in this tense dialogue between Macbeth and his wife. Macbeth carries the daggers he has used to kill the king. He has blood on his hands – 'a sorry sight', he says (line 24). The mood is tense.

 Tip

When studying a play, you need to be very clear about the overall structure. For example, students studying *Macbeth* would need to appreciate how this extract fits into the overall structure of the play. This is a key scene within the play. Immediately before the extract, the murder of King Duncan has taken place off stage. After the extract comes the discovery of the murder.

19 Read the extract, taking note of the words explained for you in the margin.

Then read the extract aloud with a partner, twice, each taking a turn to play Macbeth and Lady Macbeth.

You will notice that the lines are written in verse. As with the reading of poems, only pause at the ends of lines where there is punctuation. Do not pause when reading lines that run on.

20 Consider carefully the following important aspects of performing this extract on stage:

- The visual effect of the dagger and blood when Macbeth enters
- The fast-paced dialogue in lines 14–24 and the shortness of some lines
- The effect of the knocking from line 60 to the end of the scene.

Write a brief paragraph on each bullet point, explaining how they contribute to the dramatic impact of the scene.

21 Look at the following references to blood, all of which appear in the extract:

From Macbeth:

1 *This is a sorry sight.*

2 *Will all great Neptune's ocean wash this blood*
  Clean from my hand? No: this my hand will rather
  The multitudinous seas incarnadine,
  Making the green one red.

From Lady Macbeth:

1 *… wash this filthy witness from your hand*

2 *A little water clears us of this deed.*
  How easy is it, then!

What Macbeth and Lady Macbeth say about blood reveals a good deal about their characters at this stage of the play.

▶ Write a paragraph for each character, exploring the ways in which their words reveal their attitudes towards the murder just committed.

Remember to use quotation marks for words and phrases you quote from the extract.

22 After the murder, Macbeth thinks he hears a voice call 'Sleep no more'. The table on the next page lists the metaphors Macbeth uses to describe sleep. Exploring the words Shakespeare uses here provides an insight into Macbeth's troubled mind.

Record your answers in a table like the one shown on the next page. In the right-hand column, say briefly what you think each of these metaphors means. An example is given for you.

Metaphor	Comment
Sleep that knits up the ravelled sleeve of care	
The death of each day's life	
sore labour's bath	
Balm of hurt minds	sleep provides a medicine for minds that have been harmed
great nature's second course	
Chief nourisher in life's feast	

Link

For more about metaphors and how they are used, look back at Unit 3: 'Responding to Poetry' (page 29).

Key term

A **rhetorical question** is one used for effect, requiring no answer.

▶ Explain in a one paragraph how you think this sleep imagery reveals Macbeth's disturbed state of mind.

23 Select from Macbeth's lines one example of each of the following rhetorical devices used in the extract:

- Rhetorical question
- Hyperbole
- A repeated phrase.

Comment concisely on what each example contributes to the overall effect of the extract.

24 Look at the lines from 49 to the end of the extract.
What evidence is there to suggest that Lady Macbeth is more in control of the situation than her husband?
Using bullet points, list the evidence. Start with:

- 'She tells her husband to wash the incriminating blood from his hands'.

25 Use Activities 20–24 to help you answer the following question:

How does Shakespeare make this extract so powerful and dramatic?

Write about 300 words.
Remember to:

- include brief references to the extract to support your points
- comment on the key words Shakespeare gives the characters.

Extension

Search the web for video clips, from films and stage productions, of this key moment from the play. Compare how different versions of the play present this scene.

From AS YOU LIKE IT (Act 2, Scene 7)
by William Shakespeare

All the world's a stage,
And all the men and women merely players: 140
They have their exits and their entrances
And one man in his time plays many parts,
His acts being seven ages. At first the infant,
Mewling[1] and puking[2] in the nurse's arms;
Then the whining schoolboy with his satchel   145
And shining morning face, creeping like snail
Unwillingly to school; and then the lover,
Sighing like furnace, with a woeful ballad
Made to his mistress' eyebrow; then a soldier,
Full of strange oaths and bearded like the pard[3],   150
Jealous in honour, sudden, and quick in quarrel,
Seeking the bubble 'reputation'
Even in the cannon's mouth; and then the justice[4],
In fair round belly with good capon lined,
With eyes severe and beard of formal cut,   155
Full of wise saws[5] and modern instances –
And so he plays his part; the sixth age shifts
Into the lean and slippered pantaloon[6],
With spectacles on nose and pouch on side,
His youthful hose[7] well saved – a world too wide   160
For his shrunk shank – and his big manly voice,
Turning again toward childish treble, pipes
And whistles in his sound; last scene of all
That ends this strange eventful history
Is second childishness and mere oblivion,   165
Sans[8] teeth, sans eyes, sans taste, sans everything.

1 **Mewling** crying
2 **puking** vomiting

3 **pard** leopard or panther

4 **justice** wise person

5 **saws** sayings

6 **pantaloon** stock character of a foolish old man

7 **hose** trousers

8 *Sans* without (in French)

Exploring the extract from AS YOU LIKE IT by William Shakespeare

The extract from *Macbeth* was structured in such as way as to create a powerful dramatic impact on the audience. Much of the Drama arose from the tense dialogue between Macbeth and his wife. The careful way in which the extract was structured helped to build suspense.

This extract is, by contrast, a single speech by the character Jaques from Shakespeare's play *As You Like It*. It can be studied as a stand-alone speech. The Activities which follow show the importance of analysing structure within an individual speech.

Can you identify each of the Seven Ages of Man in this picture?

26 Read Jaques' speech carefully, taking note of the words explained for you. Remember not to pause where the lines are run on.

In small groups, discuss how this speech might be performed on stage. Consider the performance from the viewpoint of a director. Make a list of points to guide the actor, referring to the following:

- Costume, make-up and hair
- Hand gestures
- Movement on stage
- A suitable tone of voice for the character
- Pace of delivery
- Use of pauses for dramatic effect.

27 Dramatists make deliberate choices about structure:

- within individual speeches (as here)
- within longer scenes
- throughout the play as a whole.

This speech shows the importance of structure within a single speech. It begins with an extended metaphor of men and women as actors or 'players'.

▶ On a copy of the speech, use annotation to comment on the use of these highlighted phrases:

All the world's a stage,
And all the men and women merely players:

They have their exits and their entrances
And one man in his time plays many parts,
His acts being seven ages.

23 The table below sets out the Seven Ages of Man, as listed by Jaques. Using a copy of the table, add your comments on the words used to describe the different 'ages'.

Number	Age	Comment on language
1	*infant*	The onomatopoeia of 'Mewling' and 'puking' gives a very unpleasant impression of babies. There is no picture of tenderness or innocence here.
2	*whining schoolboy*	
3	*lover*	
4	*soldier*	
5	*the justice*	
6	*lean and slippered pantaloon*	
7	*second childishness*	

This Activity reminds you of the importance of analysing the ways dramatists use language and structure to communicate meanings and to create particular effects.

Extension

Below are images from recent, popular films of two Shakespeare plays.

From the 1993 film of *Much Ado About Nothing*.

From the 1996 film of *Romeo and Juliet*.

Try to watch a film, or clips from a film, of a Shakespeare play you have studied. Make notes on how well you think the film presents the play. In your notes, consider these questions:

- Which moments in the film do you find particularly engaging?
- Which characters are brought most successfully to life for you?
- Which parts of the film differ from the original play?

 Further reading

Here are the titles of other plays by Shakespeare enjoyed by Cambridge IGCSE Literature students. You might like to look at extracts from two of these if you are not already studying them for a Set Texts paper. If you can find time, you might read one of them, or even see a theatre production – perhaps after your IGCSE examinations?

A Midsummer Night's Dream

Twelfth Night

As You Like It

Julius Caesar

Richard III

 # Quick recap
Responding to the structure and language of plays

These checklists provide a quick reminder of useful questions for you to ask when exploring the way dramatists use language and structure in the plays you study.

 Tip

You have learned the importance of the opening scenes of plays. You will also find it rewarding to look at the openings of particular scenes or acts.

Structure
- How effective is the opening of the play?
- How is the content within scenes organised for maximum dramatic impact?
- How does a particular extract fit into the wider context of the whole play?
- How are long speeches structured for dramatic impact?

Language
- Which words create a striking impression on the audience?
- How do literary features such as imagery and rhetorical devices contribute to dramatic effect?
- How would characters' lines sound on stage?
- How does the dramatist create distinctive voices for the characters?
- How is dialogue used to create tension or build suspense?

Developing an informed personal response

From A STREETCAR NAMED DESIRE by Tennessee Williams

In what ways do you think this image from the 1951 film of *A Streetcar Named Desire* shows the tension between the characters of Stanley, Blanche and Stella?

[*There is a pause.*]

BLANCHE   May I – speak – *plainly*?

STELLA   Yes, do. Go ahead. As plainly as you want to.

[*Outside a train approaches. They are silent till the noise subsides. They are both in the bedroom.*   5

Under cover of the train's noises STANLEY *enters from outside. He stands unseen by the women, holding some packages in his arms, and overhears their following conversation. He wears an undershirt and grease-stained seersucker* pants.*]

*seersucker – thin cotton fabric

BLANCHE   Well – if you'll forgive me – he's *common*!   10

STELLA   Why, yes, I suppose he is.

BLANCHE   Suppose! You can't have forgotten that much of our bringing up, Stella, that you just *suppose* that any part of a gentleman's in his nature! *Not one particle, no!* Oh, if he was just – *ordinary*! Just *plain* – but good and wholesome,   15 but – *no*. There's something downright – *bestial* – about him! You're hating me saying this, aren't you?

STELLA   [*coldly*] Go on and say it all, Blanche.

BLANCHE   He acts like an animal, has an animal's habits! Eats like one, moves like one, talks like one! There's even 20 something – sub-human – something not quite to the stage of humanity yet! Yes, something – ape-like about him, like one of those pictures I've seen in – anthropological studies! Thousands and thousands of years have passed him right by and there he is – Stanley Kowalski – survivor 25 of the Stone Age! Bearing the raw meat home from the kill in the jungle! And you – *you* here – *waiting* for him! Maybe he'll strike you or maybe grunt and kiss you! That is, if kisses have been discovered yet! Night falls and the other apes gather! There in the front of the cave, all grunting 30 like him, and swilling and gnawing and hulking! His poker night! – you call it – this party of apes! Somebody growls – some creature snatches at something – the fight is on! *God*! Maybe we are a long way from being made in God's image, but Stella – my sister – there has been 35 *some* progress since then! Such things as art – as poetry and music – such kinds of new light have come into the world since then! In some kinds of people some tenderer feelings have had some little beginning! That we have got to make *grow*! And *cling* to, and hold as our flag! In this 40 dark march toward whatever it is we're approaching … *Don't – don't hang back with the brutes*!

[*Another train passes outside.* STANLEY *hesitates, licking his lips. Then suddenly he turns stealthily about and withdraws through the front door. The women are still unaware of his presence. When the train has passed he* 45 *calls through the closed front door.*]

STANLEY   Hey! Hey! Stella!

STELLA   [*who has listened gravely to* BLANCHE]: Stanley!

BLANCHE   Stell, I –

[*But* STELLA *has gone to the front door.* STANLEY *enters casually with his* 50 *packages.*]

STANLEY   Hiyuh, Stella, Blanche back?

STELLA   Yes, she's back.

STANLEY   Hiyuh, Blanche. [*He grins at her.*]

STELLA   You must've got under the car. 55

STANLEY   Them darn mechanics at Fritz's don't know their can from third base!

[*Stella has embraced him with both arms, fiercely, and full in the view of* BLANCHE. *He laughs and clasps her head to him. Over her head he grins through the curtains at* BLANCHE.

As the lights fade away, with a lingering brightness on their embrace, the music of the 'blue piano' and trumpet and drums is heard.]

60

Exploring the extract from A STREETCAR NAMED DESIRE by Tennessee Williams

In this extract from Tennessee Williams' *A Streetcar Named Desire*, Blanche is talking to her sister Stella. They are both unaware that Stella's husband, Stanley, can hear every insulting word that Blanche uses about him.

The following activities help you to develop an informed personal response to this powerful dramatic extract.

29 Read the extract carefully, keeping the following Cambridge IGCSE exam-style question in mind as you read:

Explore the ways in which Williams makes this extract such a powerfully dramatic moment.

30 Look again at the stage directions in this extract. On a copy of the extract, highlight the following:

- References to sounds, including music
- Descriptions of Stanley
- References to lighting.

Annotate your copy of the extract, commenting briefly on how these features add to the dramatic impact of the scene.

31 Look at lines 10–42.
On your copy of the extract, use a different colour from the one used in Activity 30 to highlight the words Blanche uses to describe Stanley.

Using brief annotations, comment on the dramatic effects of the words she uses.

32 Use a third colour to highlight words which help to shape *your* response to Stella in this scene. Look at:

- the words she uses
- the final stage direction.

Using brief annotations, comment on the dramatic effects that these produce.

33 Draw a mind map with the words 'Powerfully dramatic' in the middle. Use material from your answers to Activities 30–33, together with any other relevant points.

Then spend 40 minutes writing an extended response to the following question:

Explore the ways in which Williams makes this extract such a powerfully dramatic moment.

 Further reading

The following are among the plays that have been enjoyed and studied by Cambridge IGCSE students. You might like to look at extracts from two of these if you are not already studying them for a Set Texts paper. If you can find time, you might read one of them – perhaps after your IGCSE examinations?

An Ideal Husband by Oscar Wilde
Journey's End by R.C. Sherriff
A View from the Bridge by Arthur Miller
A Raisin in the Sun by Lorraine Hansberry
My Mother Said I Never Should by Charlotte Keatley
'Master Harold' … and the boys by Athol Fugard

Images from stage productions of *A View from the Bridge* (left) and *A Raisin in the Sun* (right).

 # Quick recap
Developing an informed personal response

It is not always possible to see a play you are studying performed on stage. However, it is possible to see film adaptations of many plays which are set for the Cambridge IGCSE Literature syllabus. All the extracts in this unit are from plays which have been filmed. Most will be available on DVD. Clips of many key scenes from plays can be found on the internet. These can provide a useful insight into interpretations of character, and can therefore enhance your study.

The most convincing informed responses to plays engage with the texts as Drama. It is clear from students' writing that they are discussing a

Tip

For your examination Drama set text, you should have your own notes on the areas in this checklist.

text created for performance on stage. Perceptive 'readers' of plays see the action and hear the lines spoken in the same way as a member of an audience would.

Checklist for Drama texts

Think about how dramatists:

- begin their play
- establish setting
- use stage directions
- structure their content
- present themes
- convey distinctive voices for characters
- present tensions or conflict between characters
- convey mood and shifts in mood
- use imagery and rhetorical devices.

Unit summary

In this Unit you have built on the skills of close reading developed in both the Poetry and Prose Units. You have made use once more of active learning skills such as highlighting, annotation, lists, tables and mind maps. For Drama texts, you have recognised the need to analyse both the content of plays and the special techniques dramatists use. You have explored the ways in which dramatists present characters and themes, and establish setting and mood. As with the Poetry and Prose texts, you understand the need to comment on the effects of writers' use of language such as imagery and rhetorical devices.

You have learned about the importance of the structure of key speeches and scenes, and the position of scenes within the whole play. Looking at such areas helps you to develop a detailed appreciation of the way dramatists present their subject matter for performance on a stage.

The Activities in this Unit have been designed to help you develop your independent responses to the ways in which dramatists write plays intended for performance. This Unit has stressed the importance of visualising what happens on stage, and listening to the words the characters speak. Approaching the study of plays in this way allows you to consider the dramatic impact of key speeches and scenes.

The next Unit will look in greater detail at ways of developing your writing skills as you respond to literary texts.

UNIT 6 Developing effective writing skills

Objectives

In this Unit, you will:

- develop skills required for critical writing
- develop skills required for empathic writing
- practise using quotation to support critical responses.

Tip

For a 45-minute question on a set exam text, you should spend no more than 5 minutes reading the question and doing a brief plan. This is before you start writing your answer.

In the 75-minute Unseen Paper, you should spend no more than 20 minutes reading your chosen text and doing a brief plan.

If you are taking Coursework you are likely to have considerably more time for reading and planning.

Link

If you are following the Coursework option, you will, of course, have more time to devote to planning. You should certainly make use of the opportunity. You can find out more about planning your Coursework in Unit 9.

In this Unit you will work through a number of Activities which will help you to become more confident in writing extended answers to Literature questions.

The first section of the Unit will focus on critical, or analytical, responses to poetry. The second section will focus on empathic responses to one Drama text and one Prose text.

The following paragraphs will help you understand the objectives of this Unit in more detail, and explain how the Unit will develop the skills you need when writing answers to Literature questions.

Developing skills required for critical writing

Whatever the question you are answering, you will need to write a plan. A useful plan should have two parts:

1 Gathering ideas for your answer
2 Organising your ideas in a logical order.

Writing which has not been planned can often appear rambling and can lack a clear focus. So it makes good sense to allocate some time to planning. You can then start writing with confidence. Sometimes, as you are writing your answer, you may find that you move from your original plan. This should not worry you. A plan provides a good starting-point for your writing, but you should feel free to change your mind about the direction of your answer if you have a good reason for doing so.

Critical writing is analytical. This means that you have to:

- give your own views
- support your views with evidence from the text
- comment on the effects of particular words used by the writer.

Questions requiring critical writing will ask you to consider how the writer presents a particular aspect of a text. All questions will make some reference to writers and how they communicate important aspects of the text to readers. These questions may ask you to consider characters or themes in prose texts, or thoughts and feelings in poems. Most important in these questions is the emphasis on the writer and their writing. You are expected to explore *how* writers write as well as *what* they write.

In the Activities that follow you will look at ways of responding critically, or analytically, to two poems.

It is important to remember that successful critical writing shows:

- a detailed understanding of the content
- a sensitive appreciation of the writer's use of language, structure and form
- an ability to use literary terms effectively
- confidence in providing an informed personal response.

Developing the skills required for empathic writing

Questions which ask for empathic writing allow you to engage more creatively with the text. In these tasks you have to adopt the voice of a particular character. Empathic writing needs to be rooted firmly in the text you have studied. You will not, for instance, be asked to invent new events or introduce new characters. You will not be rewarded for making your character do or say things which are not typical for him or her. It is important to remember that empathic writing must be true to the character as portrayed in the text.

Here is an example of the kind of empathic question you might be asked for Shakespeare's play *Macbeth*:

You are Lady Macbeth after the banquet where your husband behaved so strangely. Write your thoughts.

In the empathic Activities in this Unit, you will look at ways of responding creatively to one Prose and one Drama text.

Successful empathic responses show:

- a detailed understanding of the story from the character's point of view
- a sensitive appreciation of a voice which is suitable for the character
- confidence in providing an informed personal response.

Link

Look back to Unit 4 to find out more about writing critical responses to Prose texts.

Link

Look back to page 55 in Unit 4: 'Responding to Prose', to remind yourself of what you should do when answering an empathic question.

Tip

An empathic question is set on each Drama or Prose text in the Set Texts Papers 1, 4 and 5. You may also be asked to write an empathic response to a text if you are doing Coursework.

Tip

In critical writing, you need to focus on the ways in which writers use language and structure to convey their meanings. In empathic writing, you also show your appreciation of language and structure, but in a different way. You have to capture a realistic voice for the character at a particular point in the text.

Tip

Questions asking for critical writing often begin with 'How?' or 'In what ways?' Sometimes they begin with the command word 'Explore'. These words are used to encourage you to focus on the ways that writers convey their meanings. You can only do this if you make references to the words in the text.

Link

Questions are phrased in such a way as to encourage a detailed and informed personal response from you. Examples of questions and how to tackle them can be found in Unit 8, 'Preparing for the Set Texts Papers'.

Tip

If you cannot remember a quotation, provide a brief indirect reference to the relevant part of the text.

Remember that good empathic responses are informed by a student's detailed appreciation of the text and the characters.

Using support from the text

In critical responses, you should include many well-selected references to the text. Brief quotations can help to support the points you make. Where you cannot recall the precise quotation, you should provide a clear reference to the relevant part of the text. In order to achieve the highest marks, you then need to explore how writers use the key words in your quotations to achieve particular effects.

This Unit gives practical guidance about how to use and set out quotations in your answers. Even more important is the ability to link your quotations to analytical comment on the words writers use.

In empathic responses you will not be expected to use quotations. In fact, doing so would interrupt the flow of the voice you are trying to create. Your support from the text in empathic responses takes the form of words or phrases that the character would typically use, and the use of relevant information from the text.

Critical writing

Soldiers in the First World War wearing gas masks for protection.

DULCE ET DECORUM EST
by Wilfred Owen

Bent double, like old beggars under sacks,
Knock-kneed, coughing like hags, we cursed through sludge,
Till on the haunting flares[1] we turned our backs

1 **flares** rockets sent up to illuminate enemy targets

And towards our distant rest began to trudge.
Men marched asleep. Many had lost their boots,   5
But limped on, blood-shod. All went lame; all blind;
Drunk with fatigue; deaf even to the hoots
Of tired, outstripped Five-Nines[2] that dropped behind.

Gas! Gas! Quick, boys! – An ecstasy of fumbling:
Fitting the clumsy helmets just in time,   10
But someone still was yelling out and stumbling,
And flound'ring like a man in fire or lime[3]...
Dim, through the misty panes and thick green light,
As under a green sea, I saw him drowning.

In all my dreams, before my helpless sight,   15
He plunges at me, guttering, choking, drowning.

If in some smothering dreams, you too could pace
Behind the wagon that we flung him in,
And watch the white eyes writhing in his face,
His hanging face, like a devil's sick of sin,   20
If you could hear, at every jolt, the blood
Come gargling from the froth-corrupted lungs,
Obscene as cancer, bitter as the cud[4]
Of vile, incurable sores on innocent tongues, –
My friend, you would not tell with such high zest   25
To children ardent[5] for some desperate glory,
The old Lie: Dulce et decorum est
Pro patria mori.[6]

2 **Five-Nines** explosive shells

3 **lime** a white substance that burns

4 **cud** partly digested food regurgitated by cattle from the stomach to the mouth for further chewing

5 **ardent** eager

6 **Dulce et decorum est / Pro patria mori** 'It is sweet and proper to die for your country' (in Latin)

 **Further reading**

Find other poems by Wilfred Owen. Here are two you might start with: *Disabled* is a moving poem about the contrast between a young soldier's life before and after he is injured in the First World War; *Exposure* paints a bleak picture of soldiers in freezing conditions in the trenches during the war.

 Link

Look again at Walt Whitman's poem *Come up from the fields father* (page 37). Compare how Whitman and Owen write in different ways about the effects of war.

Working through a question on *Dulce et Decorum Est* by Wilfred Owen

Read the following Cambridge IGCSE-type question carefully, and then read the poem:

Explore the ways in which Owen powerfully conveys the horror of war in Dulce et Decorum Est.

The steps below set out an effective order for tackling questions such as this.

The following steps will help you to focus on points which are relevant to answering this IGCSE exam-style question.

Stage 1: using annotation

Annotating a poem or key passage from prose or drama texts is a very useful skill. It helps you to appreciate the detail of such texts. Annotation can help you in preparing responses for:

- critical essays on set texts during the course
- critical essays on coursework texts
- responses to unseen texts.

Remember that you have 45 minutes per question in set texts examination papers. It can be useful to annotate passages printed for passage-based examination questions. However, you should read and annotate passages quickly. You should be familiar with the material as it will be taken from a set text you have studied and revised.

Here is a copy of the poem with annotations. These sum up the content of each stanza and the 'ways' Owen communicates his ideas.

Picture of a troop of men exhausted from battle

Bent double, like old beggars under sacks,
Knock-kneed, coughing like hags, we cursed
    through sludge,
Till on the haunting flares we turned our backs
And towards our distant rest began to trudge.
Men marched asleep. Many had lost their boots
But limped on, blood-shod. All went lame; all blind;
Drunk with fatigue; deaf even to the hoots
Of tired, outstripped Five-Nines that dropped behind.

Similes showing how young men have aged after the ordeal of fighting

The mainly monosyllabic words convey the slow trudge of the soldiers + 'blood-shod' particularly horrific – the men's feet covered in their own bloo[d]

Gas attack which leaves one soldier unable to fit gas helmet

Gas! Gas! Quick, boys! – An ecstasy of fumbling,
Fitting the clumsy helmets just in time.
But someone still was yelling out and stumbling,
And flound'ring like a man in fire or lime …
Dim, through the misty panes and thick green light,
As under a green sea, I saw him drowning.

Use of direct speech sig[nals] a sudden change in mood

Focus shifts from group of men to one man's terrible suffering

Imagery of man 'drownin[g]' in the gas – heightened visual effect by repetiti[on] of 'green'

Suggests speaker cannot forget the nightmarish vision – 'helpless' shows he can see, but do nothing to help

In all my dreams, before my helpless sight,
He plunges at me, guttering, choking, drowning.

'plunges' continues the underwater imagery – meaning 'dives energetica[lly]'

If in some **smothering** dreams **you** too could pace
Behind the wagon that we **flung** him in,
And **watch the white eyes writing** in his face,
His hanging face, like a devil's sick of sin;
If you could hear, at every jolt, **the blood**
Come gargling from the froth-corrupted lungs
Obscence as cancer, bitter as the cud
Of vile, incurable sores on innocent tongues, –
My friend, you would not tell with such high zest
To children ardent for some desperate glory,
The old Lie: Dulce et decorum est
Pro patria mori.

Bitter address to 'you' – contrasting the reality of dying with the 'old Lie'

Sarcastic tone of voice

Contrast 'children' with 'old beggars' (Line 1)

Bitterness towards those believing it glorious to die for their country

'smothering' conveys idea of the suffocating nature of his dreams – pronoun 'you' used three times addressing those who have no experience of the reality of war

'flung': difficult to appreciate this is a human being

Alliteration

Shocking onomatopoeia – the idea of 'gargling' with blood

Tip

For practice essays during your course, take the opportunity to annotate poems or key pages from your Prose and Drama texts. This will help you to appreciate the detail of your set texts. If you are taking the Unseen examination paper, you will have time to annotate your chosen unseen text during the examination.

Remember to focus on key words and phrases that create a particularly striking impression on you. In Owen's poem, you should start with particular words or phrases that shock or horrify you, or perhaps make you angry.

> **Dulce et Decorum est.**
>
> Bent double, like old beggars under sacks,
> Knock-kneed, coughing like hags, we cursed through sludge,
> Till on the haunting flares we turned our backs
> And towards our distant rest began the trudge.
> Men marched asleep. Many had lost their boots
> But limped on, blood-shod. All went lame; all blind;
> Drunk with fatigue; deaf even to the hoots
> Of tired, outstripped Five-Nines that dropped behind.
>
> Then somewhere near in front: Whew...fup, fop, fup,
> Gas-shells? Or duds? We loosened masks in case, –
> And listened...Nothing...Far rumouring of Krupp.
> Then sudden poison hit us in the face.
> Gas! GAS! Quick, boys! – An ecstasy of fumbling,
> Fitting the clumsy helmets just in time;
> But someone still was yelling out and stumbling,
> And flound'ring like a man in fire or lime...
> Dim, through the misty panes and thick green light,
> As under a green sea, I saw him drowning.
>
> In all my dreams, before my helpless sight,
> He plunges at me, guttering, choking, drowning.

This draft of the poem shows some of the revisions Owen made to particular words and lines. Why do you think he made these changes?

Stage 2: creating a plan

Before you start writing your response in full, it is always helpful to do a plan. The annotation stage helped you to look closely at the relevant detail for your answer. A plan will help you to sort out and arrange the information in a logical order. The plan should be concise. It is there to guide you through your extended response to the question.

Here is mind map which sets out a plan for an answer to the question on *Dulce et Decorum Est*:

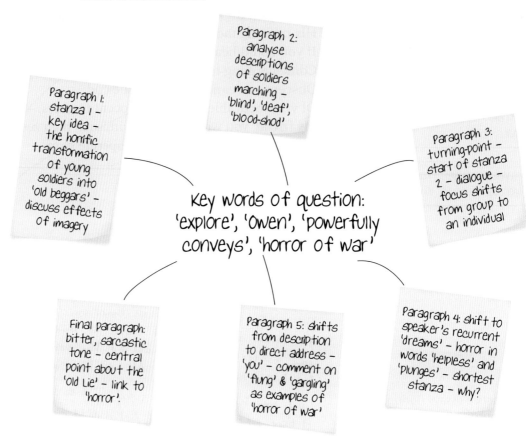

Paragraph 2: analyse descriptions of soldiers marching – 'blind', 'deaf', 'blood-shod'

Paragraph 1: stanza 1 – key idea – the horrific transformation of young soldiers into 'old beggars' – discuss effects of imagery

Paragraph 3: turning-point – start of stanza 2 – dialogue – focus shifts from group to an individual

Key words of question: 'explore', 'Owen', 'powerfully conveys', 'horror of war'

Final paragraph: bitter, sarcastic tone – central point about the 'old Lie' – link to 'horror'.

Paragraph 5: shifts from description to direct address – 'you' – comment on 'flung' & 'gargling' as examples of 'horror of war'

Paragraph 4: shift to speaker's recurrent 'dreams' – horror in words 'helpless' and 'plunges' – shortest stanza – why?

Examples of students' responses

Here are two extracts from students' responses to the question on *Dulce et Decorum Est*. An examiner's comments are added in the margin and at the end of each extract.

The response begins with background about Owen rather than directly answering the question. This may be interesting but is not really relevant to the question.

The title of the poem is not punctuated. Italics in typescript (or underlining in handwriting) can be used to indicate the title.

It should be 'Owen', and not 'Wilfred'.

Student A's response

Owen is a very famous poet who wrote poems about the First World War. One of his most famous poems is Dulce et Decorum Est. He writes very powerfully about the horror of war. He uses similes, metaphors, onomatopoeia and monosyllables to name a few devices. In the first stanza Wilfred describes the soldiers as old beggars: 'like old beggars under sacks'. He also uses a metaphor of 'drunk with fatigue', which means they were drunk with extreme tiredness.

The list of general terms may well be true, but there should be more specific comment on the effect of particular words.

The question is addressed in the third sentence but not again until the final sentence.

The quotation is not really needed, as it simply repeats the point about beggars.

The student spots that 'drunk with fatigue' is a metaphor but gives a simple explanation rather than detailed analysis.

The second paragraph simply re-tells the story of the poem. Another metaphor is spotted, but its effect is not commented on.

The use of onomatopoeia in 'gargling' is recognised but the comments are very general: 'effective'; 'you feel as if you are there'; 'The writing draws you in'.

The tone of the poem's last few lines is understood ('the poem ends in a sarcastic way'), but there is no supporting reference.

Then there was panic as they tried to fit their gas helmets. One of the soldiers didn't manage to fit his. It says he was drowning under a green sea. This is a metaphor. In the next stanza Owen talks about his nightmare of seeing the young man die – 'all his dreams'. We can all sympathise with Owen here, as we all know what it is like to have nightmares.

The fact that everyone occasionally has nightmares may be true, but does little to advance the analysis.

Owen's use of onomatopoeia 'blood gargling' is a very effective way of involving the reader. When the soldier is flung in the wagon, you feel as if you are there. The writing draws you in. Owen quotes:

The writing is Owen's; the quotation is the student's.

And watch the white eyes writhing in his face,
His hanging face, like a devil's sick of sin;
If you could hear, at every jolt, the blood
Come gargling from the froth-corrupted lungs.

Long quotations are not very helpful. The lines here are simply copied out, with no analysis of why the writer has chosen particular words to achieve his intended effects.

The poem ends in a very sarcastic way. The soldiers enlisted in the army to fight for their country. They were young and they were told it was sort of cool to fight and even die for your country. Owen's poem has proved that it is definitely not! Thus Owen shows the horror of war.

The last sentence refers to the wording of the question, and suggests that it has been answered – but it hasn't.

Examiner's comments for Student A

This response shows some understanding of the poem and makes some use of quotation. However, the comments tend to be rather general and descriptive. Language points are made (about metaphors and onomatopoeia) but are not developed. The answer tends to re-tell the story of the poem and describe the content. The approach is not analytical.

Student B's response

The opening paragraph clearly addresses the question, exploring the ways Owen captures the horrific effect of war on the soldiers. Quotations are accompanied by precise analytical comment on effects.

The poem includes a good deal of shocking imagery that conveys the sheer horror of war. The simile Owen uses to describe the soldiers – 'like old beggars under sacks' – suggests perhaps that they have not slept in a proper bed or had a good meal for days. The description 'coughing hags' gives the impression of sick soldiers who have aged prematurely and grotesquely. By focusing on this transformation of the young men into 'beggars' and 'hags', Owen captures the horrific effect of war on the soldiers. The metaphor 'drunk with fatigue' paints a vivid picture of the men swaying and stumbling as if drunk from sheer exhaustion.

The men are described as marching semi-consciously. These two lines, which comprise mainly monosyllabic words, capture the soldiers' slow 'trudge':

> Men marched asleep. Many had lost their boots
> But limped on, blood-shod. All went lame; all blind.

The fact that the men are 'blind' and 'deaf' suggests that they have in some way switched off from the carnage surrounding them. The image of them walking 'shod' in their own blood powerfully illustrates the soldiers' pain and the sheer horror of their experiences in the war.

There is more close analysis of the effects of Owen's choice of words, together with a strong personal response to the powerful image of 'blood-shod'.

The beginning of the second stanza sees an abrupt turning-point. The use of direct speech in 'Gas! Gas! Quick, boys!' signals a more urgent tone, as the focus shifts from the troop of soldiers to one man and his frantic efforts to fit his helmet during a gas attack. The words 'just in time' give the impression that the soldiers have managed to fit their helmets. However, the use of the word 'But' in the following line shows that this is not the case. Owen writes:

> But someone still was yelling out and stumbling.

The images of burning ('flound'ring like a man in fire or lime') and drowning ('As under a green sea') graphically convey the horror of this man's death.

The mention of the abrupt turning-point shows an appreciation of the poem's structure. The shift in focus from stanza to stanza is clearly charted in the rest of the essay. The change to an 'urgent tone' is recognised.

The focus shifts again in the third stanza, which is made more emphatic by being the shortest stanza. The speaker's words 'In all my dreams' indicate how his sleep is disturbed by recurring nightmares. My sympathy for the speaker is increased because the experience was so traumatic for him. He seems to feel guilty that he was not able to come to the assistance of the 'helpless' soldier. The verb 'plunges' (meaning 'dives energetically') follows the imagery of 'drowning' – it captures the man's desperate appeal for help. The horrific description of the man's last moments 'guttering, choking, drowning' makes the point all too clearly that dying in battle is not 'dulce et decorum est', the point Owen makes at the end of the poem.

The personal response to the poem is made convincing by the close attention paid to words (such as 'helpless' and 'plunges') and their effects. The images of burning and drowning are explicitly linked to one of the question's key words – 'horror'.

The description in the first three stanzas gives way to direct address in the final stanza. The reader ('you') is brought face to face with the shocking reality of war. The soldier himself is 'flung' without ceremony into a wagon. It is almost as if his fellow soldiers have become accustomed to the routine violence and death around them. The speaker does not spare any horrific detail: I think the most horrific is found in the onomatopoeia of the blood 'gargling' from his lungs at 'every jolt' of the wagon.

The shift from description to the direct address to 'you' is explored, as is the horrific effect of words such as 'flung' and 'gargling'.

Given the horrors the speaker has witnessed, the bitter tone of some of the words is not surprising. The speaker's sarcasm can be clearly heard in the address to 'My friend' towards the end of the poem. The speaker is blaming all those who have encouraged gullible young men ('ardent for some desperate glory') to fight for their country. For the speaker, who has experienced the horror of war first-hand, the idea that it is 'dulce' or 'decorum' to die for one's country is emphatically 'The Old Lie'.

The content and tone of the last few lines are convincingly analysed in the context of the question's key words 'horror of war'.

Examiner's comments for Student B

The first paragraph focuses clearly on the question ('Owen captures the horrific effect of war'), and this focus is maintained throughout the answer. There is a strong sense of a personal engagement with both the poem and question. Quotations are used to support points, and as a starting-point for further comment. Overall, this is a well-developed and detailed response, which analyses the poem convincingly. The exploration of how Owen uses language and structure to convey his meanings is sustained confidently throughout the answer.

A closer look at essay technique

The following is a list of the skills you will need to demonstrate in a critical essay:

- Responding to the question
- Showing a clear and detailed understanding of the text
- Developing points clearly
- Using an appropriate register
- Using literary terms
- Using evidence from the text to support your views.

We will now look more closely at each of these skills in turn.

Responding to the question

You must pay close attention to the key words of the question. Sometimes students forget to do this. For example, they see the title of a poem they have studied in the question, and write everything they know about that poem. But an answer requires more than just knowledge of the poem. It needs to provide a convincing and relevant response to the actual question set. This is why it is important to read the question carefully and to do a plan before writing your answer. Keep the question clearly in focus as you write your answer. There is no credit given for including material that is not relevant to the question.

Some students ignore the question completely and simply re-tell the story of the text, whether it is a poem, play, novel or short story. Such narrative responses make frequent use of connectives such as 'Next' or 'Then'. These words are tell-tale signs that the student is not answering the question but simply re-telling the story.

Students might be tempted to re-use prepared answers on a particular character or theme because they have tackled a similar question previously. But this is not a good idea. Material you might have used in previous essays needs to be re-worked to meet the particular demands of the new question you are answering.

Tip

In the question on Owen's *Dulce et Decorum Est*, you were asked to 'explore the ways' in which Owen 'powerfully conveys' the horror of war. These words are there to direct you to focus on the writing: for example, how Owen uses language and structure to communicate his feelings.

Tip

Questions will require you to focus on the text. It is always important and interesting to know when writers lived and to know something about the times in which they lived. But the main focus in questions will be on your response to the text. You will not be given marks for writing about the background of writers' lives or the times in which they lived. Always stick to the text.

Tip

The form of *Dulce et Decorum Est* is of course poetry. So you must make it clear in your writing that you are responding to a particular type of writing – a poem, written by a poet. Poets do things differently from dramatists and prose fiction writers.

Showing a clear and detailed understanding

A few straightforward comments that show a general understanding will not be enough. You must convince the examiner that you have a clear grasp of the detail in the text you are writing about. The annotation of Owen's poem demonstrated how useful this process can be for getting to grips with the detail of a text.

An understanding of the content of a particular text is never sufficient in a critical essay. You will need to show that you have carefully explored the ways in which the writer uses language, structure and form to communicate what they have to say.

Showing a detailed understanding is not the same as writing down every point you could make about a particular text. You must be selective. Choose the best material for your answer. In examination essays on set texts you have only 45 minutes, so you cannot write about everything. In Coursework, you should not write excessively long essays. So select the material that most effectively answers the question you have been set.

Developing points clearly

Your points must be carefully organised into paragraphs so that one point leads logically to the next. The planning stage is useful for helping you to sort out a sensible order for the points you want to make. Every sentence you write should be relevant to the question that has been set. The logic of your argument should be clear throughout the answer.

It is not necessary to write a long introduction, telling your reader what you intend to do in the essay. It is best to engage with the key words of the question straight away, and move to your first specific point. There is no credit for starting essays with 'courtesy' introductions such as 'In this essay I am going to write about ...'

You should make your points concisely and move on. There is no credit for repeated points or for 'padding out' your answer.

You need to make your reader's job a pleasure and not a chore. Remember the following:

* Organise your paragraphs logically
* Check that spelling, punctuation and grammar are accurate
* Write legibly so that your reader can easily follow your ideas.

Using an appropriate register

Writing in critical essays should be formal. You should not, for example, use contractions such as *isn't* or *didn't* in formal writing. Your personal response should not include slang or colloquial English. Here are some examples of an inappropriate **register**:

Key term

Register refers to the level of formality in writing. Critical essays should avoid informal English unless you are quoting from a text.

- Lady Macbeth wears the trousers in her marriage.
- Shakespeare presents Tybalt as a cool dude.
- Romeo and Juliet are an item.
- Piggy has issues with obesity.
- Tom Robinson was not in a happy place.

Using literary terms

The more common literary terms found in this book can be helpful in making points concisely.

There are, however, two things to avoid:

Tip

Remember: explaining why a writer uses particular words or sounds is more important than simply using a particular literary term.

- Merely spotting or labelling literary devices: for example, 'This is a metaphor. It means ...'
- Using literary terms instead of commenting on how writers create certain effects: for example, 'Line 17 contains stichomythia'.

A more appropriate way of incorporating literary terms can be seen in the following example:

The metaphor 'drunk with fatigue' paints a vivid picture of the men swaying and stumbling as if drunk from sheer exhaustion.

Here, the term 'metaphor' is used to support the comment on the language used by the writer to create particular effects. Your job is to show why a writer uses a particular device and what effect it has on you, as the reader. The brief example above offers a response to the writer's words that has moved beyond simple description to analysis.

Tip

A useful 'formula' to remember for critical writing is:

POINT + QUOTATION + COMMENT = ANALYSIS

Using evidence from the text to support your views

Student B's writing on *Dulce et Decorum Est* provides good examples of how to use quotations effectively. Look carefully at the following:

1 The use of direct speech in 'Gas! Gas! Quick, boys!' signals a more urgent tone, as the focus shifts from the troop of soldiers to one man and his frantic efforts to fit his helmet during a gas attack.
2 The speaker's sarcasm can be clearly heard in the address to 'My friend' towards the end of the poem. The speaker is blaming all those who have encouraged gullible young men ('ardent for some desperate glory') to fight for their country.

In each of these examples, the student:

- makes a *point*
- supports the point with a *quotation*
- provides a *comment* on the key words in the quotation.

This approach is a useful one to follow. Note that the original point is supported, and the quotation is followed by precise comment on the effects of particular words. The comments which *follow* points and quotations are the key to good analysis.

Quotations: some common mistakes

For quotations to be useful in supporting your response, they should be as brief as possible and integrated smoothly into your sentences. The proper handling of textual evidence indicates a high-level response.

Here are some common errors that students make in using quotations.

Link

Look again at the two examples of student writing in response to the question on *Dulce et Decorum Est.* The points made by Student A were general and descriptive. The points made by Student B were precise and analytical.

Quotation error	What is wrong with this?
Using long, unfocused quotations	Such an approach gets in the way of commenting on key words. Long quotations often seem to be 'space fillers'.
Quoting without making a comment on key words in the quotation	Quoting on its own is not sufficient when you are analysing literature. The quotation should lead to analytical comment.
Making a point and then writing out a quotation – without making the connection clear	It is important to integrate the quotation smoothly into your own sentences. In this way your reader can follow the link between point and quotation.
Not exploring the key word(s) in quotations	Close analysis of the key words you quote is necessary for the higher grades.
Explaining what quotations mean	There is no point in simply repeating what is in the quotation. This is description rather than analysis.

Critical writing practice

Working through the previous section of this Unit will have helped you to become more confident in writing responses to Literature questions. You have been introduced to the writing skills you will need, from annotating your text to planning your answer, as well as useful essay techniques. This section now gives you the opportunity to put what you have learned so far into practice, by attempting an answer to an example essay question.

FARMHAND

by James K. Baxter

You will see him light a cigarette
At the hall door careless, leaning his back
Against the wall, or telling some new joke
To a friend, or looking out into the secret night.

But always his eyes turn   5
To the dance floor and the girls drifting like flowers
Before the music that tears
Slowly in his mind an old wound open.

His red sunburnt face and hairy hands
Were not made for dancing or love-making   10
But rather the earth wave breaking
To the plough, and crops slow-growing as his mind.

He has no girl to run her fingers through
His sandy hair, and giggle at his side
When Sunday couples walk. Instead   15
He has his awkward hopes, his envious dreams to yarn[1] to.

But ah in harvest watch him
Forking stooks[2], effortless and strong –
Or listening like a lover to the song
Clear, without fault, of a new tractor engine.   20

1 **yarn** spin thread (or a story)
2 **stooks** bundles of hay

The previous section of this Unit guided you through a response to a poem
by Wilfred Owen. The order went like this:

Read the poem and the question

Annotate the poem for content **and** for the ways the poet
communicates the content

Gather ideas in the form of a mind map

Do a paragraph plan

Write the essay

Further practice

You now have the opportunity to practise these critical writing skills for yourself.

Read the poem *Farmhand* carefully, with the following question in mind:

In what ways does Baxter make the farmhand such a moving figure in the poem?

Use the flowchart on the previous page to remind you and guide you through your response from first reading to final essay.

Quick recap
Writing critical essays

Here is a checklist to help you when writing critical essays.

- Read the question carefully and note its key words.
- Know the text in detail so you have enough material to write about.
- Draw a mind map to help you select relevant material.
- Write a brief plan to help you arrange your material in a logical order.
- Answer the question set, making sure every sentence is relevant.
- Be selective, as you cannot write about everything in the time available.
- Use detail from the text to support your points.
- Integrate brief quotations smoothly into your own writing.
- Analyse key words in your quotations, showing how writers achieve their effects.
- Remember the importance of effective paragraphing.
- Consider the needs of the reader by writing legibly, in clear and accurate English.

 # Writing empathic responses

This section provides guidance on how to respond to empathic questions.

Go back to pages 98–100 and re-read the extract from Tennessee Williams' *The Glass Menagerie*. As you read the extract again, consider the following empathic question:

You are Tom later that day thinking about the row with your mother.
Write your thoughts.

The steps that follow set out an effective order for approaching empathic questions such as this.

Step 1: Draw a mind map

Draw a mind map with the words 'Tom after the row' in the middle.

Then read carefully the relevant parts of the text for useful material for your answer. As you do so, add to your mind map any thoughts that Tom is likely to have at this moment. A mind map for this question might look like this:

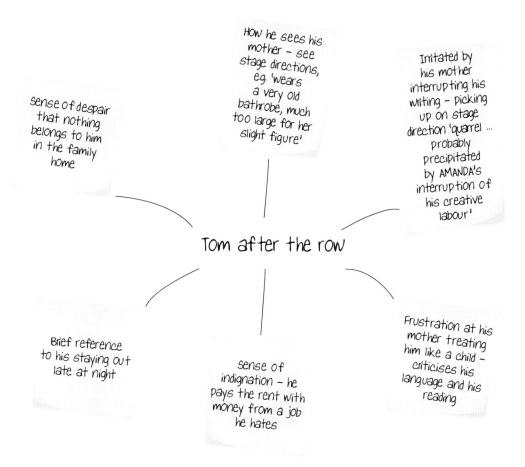

How he sees his mother – see stage directions, e.g. 'wears a very old bathrobe, much too large for her slight figure'

sense of despair that nothing belongs to him in the family home

Irritated by his mother interrupting his writing – picking up on stage direction 'quarrel ... probably precipitated by AMANDA'S interruption of his creative labour'

Tom after the row

Brief reference to his staying out late at night

sense of indignation – he pays the rent with money from a job he hates

Frustration at his mother treating him like a child – criticises his language and his reading

 Link

This type of mind map provides a very important brainstorming activity when empathic questions relate to characters from longer texts, such as plays and novels. Later in this Unit, on pages 148–49, you will find a checklist that is useful when dealing with characters for set examination or Coursework texts.

Stage 2: Write a plan

The mind map helps to gather your thoughts, or rather the character's thoughts. Next you should arrange these thoughts into a writing plan – a logical order for the character at the point in the text given in the question. A list such as this provides an effective way of ordering your empathic response. Look at the following example.

How the row started with his mother interrupting Tom's work

How his mother appeared to him

The way she treats him as child

His anger at lack of both privacy and possessions

His attitude towards factory work and his creative writing

End on unhappy note, with reference to his staying out late

Examples of students' responses

Here are some extracts from students' responses to the question, together with comments from an examiner.

Example 1:
If I were Tom, I would begin by saying how angry my mother made me.

Examiner's comment
This is an incorrect approach. The student should write in Tom's own voice, right from the start.

Example 2:
Oh my God! My mother is just so not appreciating my own life here. So she wants me listen to her. Don't think so.

Examiner's comment
Using modern expressions that the character would not have used can be distracting. The voice of the character suffers as a consequence.

Example 3:
Consequently there she appeared in front of me, the very image of a demented virago. Her Gorgon-like demeanour would freeze any person unfortunate enough to meet her steely gaze.

Examiner's comment
This student is aiming to impress with some adventurous vocabulary. The reference to Gorgon is apt enough: a terrifying woman (from Greek mythology) whose gaze turned those who looked at her into stone. However, the voice here is not a convincing voice for Tom.

Example 4:

She treats me like a child. For example: 'What's the matter with you, you – big – big IDIOT!'

Examiner's comment

The first sentence is true enough, and it is expressed in a voice which is suitable for Tom. But the second sentence, with its direct quotation, is more suitable for a critical essay rather than an empathic response. The 'for example' has the effect of interrupting the flow of the character's voice.

Example 5:

Every day is the same. I've had it up to here! In she comes every morning with her screeching 'Rise and shine!' Well, today was the last straw. The only time I had to myself to do just a little writing in the privacy of my room. Is it wrong to ask for just a little peace and quiet? What with the work in the factory I don't exactly have a luxury of time to call my own.

So there she stands in her metal curlers and ancient bathrobe. Such a loud voice in such a tiny body. So I knock over the chair and ask her what in Christ's name she thinks she's doing barging into the only sanctuary I have. Don't blaspheme, she says. Big IDIOT, she's shouts at me. Why, if it weren't for me, she'd have no roof over her head. And yet there she is all the time: 'Don't say that', 'Don't do this', and 'Don't you dare ...'

Well, I'm through with being treated like a child. I'm a slave sure enough at the factory. But I'm through with being a slave in this crummy house. Home, sweet home! I have absolutely nothing here I *could* call my home. Why, I can't even read the books I want to. That hideous book by that insane Mr Lawrence. Who on earth does she think she is? Humiliating me by taking my books back to the library ... I spend almost every waking hour in that goddam Continental Shoemakers. Is that to be my life? Fifty-five years under fluorescent tubes. Sure am crazy about that idea!

No. These papers on this table are my real life. What I want is to write. And she will never understand that. If I don't have that dream to cling to, then let someone put me to sleep. And let's do it now. Battering my brains out would be more humane than looking forward to a lifetime's incarceration in a warehouse.

I am well and truly at the end of my patience. If I want to stay out half the night I will – movies or not. Anything to escape this hell.

Examiner's comment

This response successfully captures Tom's thoughts for the given moment. He is clearly angry at his mother's constant interruptions and interference. He is frustrated by his lack of privacy and possessions. He dreams of a life of the imagination that is very different from his suffocating job at Continental Shoemakers, where Tom sees himself as a slave.

The voice is recognisably Tom's throughout the response, which is written totally from his perspective. The answer is convincingly rooted in the world of the text.

A closer look at empathic technique

In the introduction to this Unit on page 129, you were introduced to empathic questions and what sort of writing is needed for an empathic response. Re-read that section now if you feel you need to revise this information.

The skills you need to demonstrate in an empathic response are:

- Responding to the question
- Showing a clear and detailed understanding of the text
- Developing points clearly
- Assuming an appropriate voice
- Using details from the text to support your answer.

We will now look in more detail at each of these skills in turn.

Responding to the question

In empathic questions (on drama or prose texts) you assume the voice of a particular character at a specific moment in the text. Empathic questions always include the instruction *Write your thoughts*.

When responding to empathic questions you need to show a clear appreciation of the following:

- The character's perspective on events
- The character's perspective on other characters
- The moment specified in the question.

Showing a clear and detailed understanding of the text

Empathic responses must be rooted firmly in the world of the text. You are not being asked to introduce additional characters or to make existing characters behave in unusual ways. Their thoughts must be 'in character'.

You need to show a clear understanding of the following:

- What the character is like
- Events from their perspective
- The way they would be thinking at the chosen moment
- What happens leading up to this moment.

Developing points clearly

The question will specify a moment in the text for you to write the character's 'thoughts'. You will need to consider carefully the order in which you make the relevant points in your answer. This order will

Tip

The moment chosen for the character's thoughts is usually at a significant point in the text. This may be at the end of the play, novel or short story.

Tip

Atticus, the father and lawyer character in Harper Lee's novel *To Kill a Mockingbird*, has a wonderful way of expressing what empathy is: 'You never really understand a person until you consider things from his point of view – until you climb into his skin and walk around in it'. This is a useful definition of empathy, which it might be helpful to keep in mind when you approach empathic questions.

not necessarily follow the order of events in the text. The order of the character's thoughts will partly depend on the moment given in the question.

The key point you should consider here is: what is the character likely to be thinking about at that precise moment?

Assuming an appropriate voice

The tone of the voice must be suitable for the character and for the moment chosen for you to write their thoughts. You should write in the first person – so write 'I feel', not 'He feels'. Successful empathic responses include words and phrases that are typical of the character. In this way, they demonstrate their appreciation of the writing by providing echoes of the text.

Using details from the text to support your answer

This is not a critical essay. You should not use direct quotations in empathic responses, as they can interrupt the flow of the character's voice. However, you may wish the character to use phrases they have spoken in the text. This is fine, so long as it sounds like something the character might say at the moment indicated in the question. Remember not to use quotation marks!

In empathic responses, textual support is provided by the range of detail that roots your answer firmly in the world of the text.

Empathic writing practice

The previous sections of this Unit have given you guidance on how to plan and write a response to an empathic question on a character from a play. This can be summarised as shown in the flowchart below:

Re-read relevant parts of the text

Draw a mind map outlining the character's thoughts at the given moment

Write a list putting the thoughts in a clear and logical order

Write your response.

Now you have the opportunity to put into practice what you have learned about empathic writing.

Tip

Some students make the mistake of not writing in character. They might begin 'If I were Lady Macbeth, my thoughts would be ...' This is an incorrect approach. Throughout the answer, you must write in the first person as if you are the character. For example, for Lady Macbeth you might begin, 'I could hardly believe the change in my husband'.

Tip

Your character may use words or phrases found in the text, but you should not put quotation marks around them. Make sure the voice sounds realistic for the character.

Go back to pages 85–91 and re-read Karl Sealy's short story *The Pieces of Silver*.

Then carefully read the following question:

You are Clement, sitting under the breadfruit tree after your family's evening meal (line 175).
Write your thoughts.

Hot-seating activity

Working in small groups, assign the role of Clement to one student. Ask questions which try to find out what Clement is thinking at the moment specified in the question.

Use the flowchart on the previous page to guide you through your response from reading the story with the question in mind, right through to writing the final response.

Read aloud your answer to a partner. Ask your partner to stop you reading when:

- you use a word or phrase not typical of the character
- you get your facts wrong
- you confuse the order of events.

Then make revisions to your answer which take the above points into account.

Tip

Empathic questions will specify a moment for the character's thoughts. In this question, the moment is after the Dovecot family's meal. Anything that happened after the meal would not be relevant in your answer.

For a question which gave the end of the story as the specified moment for Clement, the response would be significantly different.

Make up your own empathic questions on key characters from your Prose or Drama examination text.

Choose a key moment from the text.

Write your thoughts, assuming a suitable voice for the character at the moment you have chosen.

Remember that some moments in the text may not be suitable for an empathic question. For example, Romeo in the middle of fighting with Tybalt will not have time to think and reflect on his actions!

Exercises such as this provide very useful revision of the detail of the texts you are studying.

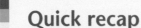

Quick recap
Writing empathic responses

1 Re-read those parts of the text which are relevant to the question.
2 Draw a mind map to display the character's thoughts:

- at that moment
- about other characters

Tip

If you wish to correct or revise your answer, cross words and phrases out and insert new words above them. If there is insufficient space, write new words or phrases at the end of your answer. Use an asterisk to indicate where you have done this.

You can find further guidance on checking your work in Unit 9, on Coursework (see page 191).

- about events relevant to them
- about other areas of importance to the character.

3   Using bullets, put in a logical order the key points you intend to make.
4   Write your response, creating a suitable voice for the character and the moment specified.
5   Check your answer, and make suitable revisions where:

- you use a word or phrase not typical of the character
- you get your facts wrong
- you confuse the order of events.

Unit summary

In this Unit you have considered in turn the skills you need for answering critical essay questions and empathic questions.

For successful critical writing, you must show a detailed understanding of relevant content. It is also essential to show a sensitive appreciation of how writers use language, structure and their chosen form.

You were reminded that literary terms are useful when used effectively as part of your analysis. They should, however, never be used merely to list or describe the devices writers use.

For successful empathic writing, you must also show a detailed understanding of content that is relevant for the character and for the moment given in the question. Empathic responses must sustain a convincing voice for the character.

Critical and empathic questions in different ways invite informed personal responses. This Unit has set out clear step-by-step guidance on how to improve your writing skills for both types of question. The Unit has built on the active learning skills introduced in earlier Units. For example, mind maps were used to gather relevant material and bullet lists to put it into a logical order.

The next three Units also put you as the active learner at the centre of your preparation for whichever of the following you are taking:

- the Set Texts Papers
- the Unseen Paper
- the Coursework component.

3 Preparing for assessment

UNIT 7 Preparing for the Unseen Paper

Objectives

In this Unit, you will:

- consider the objectives of the Unseen Paper

- develop strategies for understanding and responding to Unseen Poetry texts

- develop strategies for understanding and responding to Unseen Prose texts

- have the opportunity to do a practice IGCSE-style Unseen paper.

Link

Before beginning work on the Activities in this Unit, have another look at the Quick Recap sections in Units 3 and 4: 'Responding to Poetry' and 'Responding to Prose'.

What will you have to do for the Unseen Paper?

Here are the essential points that you need to know about the Unseen Paper:

Unseen Paper	Requirements
(Paper 3) 1 hour 15 minutes	There are *two* questions: • *one* on a single poem or extract from a longer poem • *one* on an extract from a Prose text. For this paper you must answer just *one* question.

You should also remember the following points about the Unseen Paper:

1 After the main question, bullet points are provided to help you answer the question.
2 Questions on this paper require critical writing. Empathic questions are not set.
3 Questions are not set on Drama texts for the Unseen Paper.
4 You should spend about 20 minutes reading the question paper and planning your answer.
5 The meanings of difficult words will be given.

What skills will be tested in the Unseen Paper?

Whether you decide to answer the Poetry or Prose question, certain objectives are common to both. Whichever question you choose to answer, you will need to show that you are able to do the following:

- Engage with the detail of your chosen text as you answer the question
- Consider deeper meanings as well as surface meanings
- Analyse form, structure and language
- Develop an informed personal response to the text.

How to approach Unseen texts

Tip

The Unseen Paper includes 20 minutes for reading and preparation. You are not given this preparation time in a Set Texts paper, as you should already be very familiar with the content of your set texts.

Students are sometimes anxious about the Unseen Paper. They perhaps feel more confident with a Set Texts paper because they can prepare by re-reading their texts and learning their notes. However, you should remember that the skills being tested in the Unseen Paper are also tested in your critical writing in a Set Texts paper. This should be reassuring for you, since it means that you will be practising the same skills of critical analysis throughout your course.

Remember that the examiner will be aware that the texts are unfamiliar to you, and will mark your work with that in mind. The examiner is likely to accept your ideas and interpretations if they are supported by relevant evidence from the text.

Because you do not know the chosen texts for the Unseen Paper, you have to think on your feet. This can in turn lead you to produce writing which includes original and fresh insights. There are, of course, no study guides to read in order to prepare for this paper. Whilst there is no correct answer, you must present your views convincingly, providing support from the text.

This Unit introduces you to the particular features of Unseen questions, and offers guidance about how to respond to them effectively.

The following flowchart sets out guidance which is relevant whether you attempt the Poetry or the Prose option for your Unseen question.

Spend about 15 minutes reading and annotating your chosen question and passage

Spend about 5 minutes writing a plan before starting your answer

Answer the question set, and do not resort to just telling the story or describing the content

Focus on the *how* the writer uses form, structure and language as well as the content of the text

Use the 'Point + Quotation + Comment' strategy to explore the detail of the text

Leave about 5 minutes to check your writing

The next two sections of this Unit will suggest how you should tackle Unseen questions for first Poetry and then Prose. You will then have the opportunity to attempt a practice Unseen paper.

Understanding and responding to Poetry texts

Link

Remember that in Unit 3: 'Responding to Poetry', you considered the following points when exploring poems:

- Words appealing to the senses
- Imagery
- Sound
- Rhetorical features
- Structure
- Mood.

You should consider the same points when analysing poetry for the Unseen Paper.

Read the following question, and then the poem which follows it:

How does the poet present to you the speaker's changing attitude towards Mary as you read the poem?

To help you answer this question, you might consider the following:

- The poet's memories of her early friendship with Mary and also Mary's moving to a new neighbourhood
- The poet's attitude towards Mary as she sits near her on the bus
- The ways in which the poet creates a particular voice for the speaker.

THE CHOOSING

We were first equal, Mary and I
with same coloured ribbons in mouse-coloured hair
and with equal shyness,
we curtseyed to the lady councillor[1]
for copies of Collins' Children's Classics.   5
First equal, equally proud.

Best friends too Mary and I
a common bond in being cleverest (equal)
in our small school's small class.
I remember   10
the competition for top desk
at school service.
And my terrible fear
of her superiority at sums.

I remember the housing scheme[2]   15
where we both stayed.
The same houses, different homes,
where the choices were made.

I don't know exactly why they moved,
but anyway they went.   20
Something about a three-apartment
and a cheaper rent.
But from the top deck of the high-school bus
I'd glimpse among the others on the corner
Mary's father, mufflered[3], contrasting strangely   25
with the elegant greyhounds[4] by his side.
He didn't believe in high school education,
especially for girls,
or in forking out[5] for uniforms.

Ten years later on a Saturday –   30
I am coming from the library –
sitting near me on the bus,
Mary
with a husband who is tall,
curly-haired, has eyes   35
for no one else but Mary.
Her arms are round the full-shaped vase
that is her body.
Oh, you can see where the attraction lies
in Mary's life –   40
not that I envy her, really.

1 **councillor** member of the local council

2 **housing scheme** housing estate (term used in Scotland)

3 **mufflered** wearing a scarf
4 **greyhounds** a tall, slender dog bred for their speed

5 **forking out** paying for unwillingly

And I am coming from the library
with my arms full of books.
I think of those prizes that were ours for the taking
and wonder when the choices got made   45
we don't remember making.

Tackling the Unseen Poetry question

In the Activities that follow you will use a number of strategies to help you answer this question on Unseen poetry.

A good starting-point for any response to a poem is to think carefully about your first impressions on reading the poem. Which words do you find most striking? Do you find the poem enjoyable, and why?

In the case of *The Choosing*, the following ideas might well come into your mind:

- What it might be like to be both a friend and a rival
- The unfair way in which Mary's future life is dictated by her sexist father
- The changing feelings of the speaker: anger towards the father and jealousy towards Mary.

Taking into account your own responses as you read will help you to develop an informed personal appreciation of the poem when you come to answer the question.

1 Read the poem carefully, and then look again at the question. Take note of the words explained for you.

Write down the question and highlight or underline the key words.

Read a copy of the poem, with pen in hand. This is an important part of close and active engagement with the text. As you read, keep the question in mind. Then, using different colours, annotate the following on your copy of the poem:

- Words and aspects of the poem's structure that you find particularly striking
- Words and phrases you find puzzling and need to revisit
- Details you might use to address the question's three bullet points.

Even in about 50 minutes of writing, you will not be able to say everything about the poem that might be relevant. In Unit 6: 'Developing effective writing skills', you learned how important it is to be selective. You cannot write about everything in the time available – however, try to say something in your essay in response to the three bullet points in the question.

Tip

For the Unseen Paper, you should annotate the question and poem on the question paper itself.
Keep your highlighting and annotations brief. Do not get carried away so that your page becomes a mass of confusing colour!
Do not use a highlighter when it comes to writing your answer.

2 Read the poem, paying particular attention to how the poet:

- uses imagery to achieve particular effects
- uses sound and rhythm to create a distinctive voice for the speaker
- begins, develops and ends the poem
- varies the length of stanzas and lines
- presents any contrasts.

The differences between the later lives of Mary and the speaker are at the heart of the poem. When exploring poetry, you will find it helpful to consider whether there are any differences, oppositions or contrasts in the poems you are studying. Such contrasts are often signalled by clear turning-points or twists in the poem.

3 Write a plan for your answer to the question.

You will already have begun to make judgements about the content of the poem and the writer's methods. Before starting to write your essay, you should pause to do a plan. This will help you to keep your writing on track, and make sure you answer the question. You could use either bullet points or a mind map for your plan.

Here is an example of a mind map for answering the question on *The Choosing*.

Tip

Using a mind map to plan your essay will help you to organise your paragraphs as you write. Remember the following points when using a mind map:

- You should use abbreviations to save time. In the example shown here, 'M' has been used to indicate Mary, 'paragraph' has been shortened to 'para' and language shortened to 'lang'.
- Always make sure that the points you make relate to the question.

MARY AND SPEAKER AT SCHOOL
Lang & structure of stanzas 1-3
How the poem begins
My 1st impressions of the speaker's voice

MARY LEAVES FOR NEW HOME
M's move signals a clear turning-point
Significance of M's father in stanza 4
Words used to describe his attitude to education

OVERVIEW
Opening para – brief summary of the poem's content and structure

speaker's changing attitude towards Mary

SPEAKER'S VOICE
Colloquial mainly – but also poetic
Rhythm in stanza 1 suggests equal relationship
Short lines stand out
Lines particularly memorable for the voice

MARY ON BUS
Lang & structure of final 2 stanzas
Description of M
speaker's feelings now – especially in final stanza

As a reminder of what makes a successful piece of critical writing, look again at the 'Quick recap' on page 142 in Unit 6: 'Developing effective writing skills'.

Remember: it is more important to explore words and their effects than to use literary terms which simply describe the devices writers use.

Critical responses which are awarded high marks pay close attention to the effects created by individual words and phrases.

Writing your answer

In your critical writing you will need to demonstrate the following:

- A detailed understanding of the content
- A sensitive appreciation of the writer's use of language, structure and form
- An ability to use literary terms effectively
- Confidence in providing an informed personal response.

Using your annotated copy of the poem and the mind map as a starting-point, write your answer to the question on *The Choosing*. Spend 50 minutes writing, and a final 5 minutes checking what you have written.

Time for reflection

After you have finished writing your essay, consider which of the following comments best describes the way you answered the question:

- I ran out of time and could not write all I had to say in response to the question.
- I used all the time available to develop a detailed argument, and left 5 minutes to check what I had written.
- I ran out of things to say some time before the end.

If you ran out of time, you were probably a little too ambitious in planning your answer, and included too many points. Remember that you cannot mention all possible points in the time available. It is better to develop fewer points in greater detail than to include too many. Students making too many points leave themselves insufficient time to develop their ideas or sustain their analysis.

Students finishing before the end of the exam often fail to develop their points in sufficient detail. Their analysis of words tends to be rather brief and under-developed.

An important part of active learning means reflecting on how you perform, as you have done for this example of a poetry Unseen question. You should reflect on what went well and what went less well. Evaluation of this kind helps you to perform better next time.

Consider the following questions when evaluating and improving your performance:

- Did I get the timing right or wrong?
- Was my plan sufficiently detailed?
- Did I keep glancing back at the question and plan to check that I was on track?
- Did I follow the 'Point + Quotation + Comment' strategy?

Understanding and responding to Prose texts

Link

In Unit 4: 'Responding to Prose' you considered the following points when exploring Prose texts:

- How characters are portrayed
- How ideas or themes are presented
- How mood is conveyed
- How narrative viewpoint is established.

Read carefully the following extract in which Miss Brodie is telling her pupils about her engagement to a man who died during the First World War.

How does the writer strikingly portray Miss Brodie and her relationship with other characters in the passage?

To help you answer this question, you might consider:

- your impressions of Miss Brodie as you read the passage
- the way Miss Brodie interacts with her pupils and with Miss Mackay
- the way in which the writer uses dialogue.

Now read the passage carefully, bearing in mind the above points.

'If anyone comes along,' said Miss Brodie, 'in the course of the following lesson, remember that it is the hour for English grammar. Meantime I will tell you a little of my life when I was younger than I am now, though six years older than the man himself.' 5

She leaned against the elm. It was one of the last autumn days when the leaves were falling in little gusts. They fell on the children who were thankful for this excuse to wriggle and for the allowable movements in brushing the leaves from their hair and laps. 10

'Season of mists and mellow fruitfulness[1]. I was engaged to a young man at the beginning of the War but he fell on Flanders' Field[2],' said Miss Brodie. 'Are you thinking, Sandy, of doing a day's washing?'

'No, Miss Brodie.' 15

'Because you have got your sleeves rolled up. I won't have to do with girls who roll up the sleeves of their blouses, however fine the weather. Roll them down at once, we are civilised beings. He fell the week before Armistice[3] was declared. He fell like an autumn leaf, although he was only twenty-two years of age. When 20 we go indoors we shall look on the map at Flanders, and the spot where my lover was laid before you were born. He was poor. He came from Ayrshire[4], a countryman, but a hard-working and clever scholar. He said, when he asked me to marry him, "We shall have to drink water and walk slow." That 25 was Hugh's country way of expressing that we would live quietly.

1 **'Season of mists and mellow fruitfulness'** the first line of Keats' poem *To Autumn*

2 **Flanders' Field** First World War battlefields in the region of Flanders, which spans southern Belgium and north-west France.

3 **Armistice** the day the First World War ended

4 **Ayrshire** a county in south-west Scotland

We shall drink water and walk slow. What does the saying signify, Rose?'

'That you would live quietly, Miss Brodie,' said Rose Stanley who six years later had a great reputation for sex.   30

The story of Miss Brodie's felled fiancé[5] was well on its way when the headmistress, Miss Mackay, was seen to approach across the lawn. Tears had already started to drop from Sandy's little pig-like eyes and Sandy's tears affected her friend Jenny, later famous in the school for her beauty, who gave a sob and   35 groped up the leg of her knickers for her handkerchief. 'Hugh was killed,' said Miss Brodie, 'a week before the Armistice. After that there was a general election and people were saying "Hang the Kaiser!" Hugh was one of the Flowers of the Forest, lying in his grave.' Rose Stanley had now begun to weep. Sandy slid her   40 wet eyes sideways, watching the advance of Miss Mackay, head and shoulders forward, across the lawn.

'I am come to see you and I have to be off,' she said. 'What are you little girls crying for?'

'They are moved by a story I have been telling them. We are   45 having a history lesson,' said Miss Brodie, catching a falling leaf neatly in her hand as she spoke.

'Crying over a story at ten years of age!' said Miss Mackay to the girls who had stragglingly risen from the benches, still dazed with Hugh the warrior. 'I am only come to see you and I must   50 be off. Well, girls, the new term has begun. I hope you all had a splendid summer holiday and I look forward to seeing your splendid essays on how you spent them. You shouldn't be crying over history at the age of ten. 'My word!'

'You did well,' said Miss Brodie to the class, when Miss Mackay   55 had gone, 'not to answer the question put to you. It is well, when in difficulties, to say never a word, neither black nor white. Speech is silver but silence is golden. Mary, are you listening? What was I saying?'

Mary Macgregor, lumpy, with merely two eyes, a nose and a   60 mouth like a snowman, who was later famous for being stupid and always to blame and who, at the age of twenty-three, lost her life in a hotel fire, ventured, 'Golden.'

'What did I say was golden?'

Mary cast her eyes around her and up above. Sandy   65 whispered, 'The falling leaves.'

'The falling leaves,' said Mary.

'Plainly,' said Miss Brodie, 'you were not listening to me. If only you small girls would listen to me I would make you the crème de la crème[6].'   70

---

5 **fiancé** man she was engaged to be married to

6 **crème de la crème** cream of the cream; the very best (French)

What does this photograph from the 1961 film of the novel reveal about the relationship between Miss Brodie and her pupils?

Link

Look again at the section on third person narration in Unit 4: 'Responding to Prose' (see page 80). In this passage the third person narrative viewpoint is close to that of Miss Brodie herself – for example, the description of Mary as 'lumpy' and 'later famous for being stupid' is one perhaps that Miss Brodie would share. It is almost as if the scene is viewed through Miss Brodie's eyes.

Tackling the Unseen Prose question

In the Activities below you will use a number of strategies to help you answer this question on Unseen Prose.

4 Read the passage carefully, and then look again at the question. Take note of the words explained for you.

Highlight or underline the key words in the question.

Read a copy of the passage, with pen in hand. As with Poetry, this is an important part of the close and active engagement with Prose fiction. As you read, keep the question in mind. Then, using different colours, annotate the following on your copy of the passage:

- Words that you find particularly striking
- Words and phrases you find puzzling and need to revisit
- Aspects of the structure you find striking
- Details you might use to address the question's three bullet points.

Remember that you will not be expected to write about everything in 50 minutes. There will be more material than you can use. So you should select material which is most useful for your answer.

5 Read the passage carefully, paying particular attention to how the writer:

- uses imagery to achieve particular effects
- uses narrative viewpoint to convey Miss Brodie's attitudes towards her pupils and Miss Mackay
- structures the writing within the extract
- changes the mood during the extract
- presents any contrasts or conflicts.

Tip

Looking at the structure of poems is relatively easy: you can see there are separate lines and perhaps separate stanzas. In Prose passages, too, it is important to consider carefully the way writers organise their content. Ask yourself the following questions:

- How does the passage begin?
- How does it develop?
- How does it end?
- How and where are dialogue and description used in the passage?

A useful way into prose fiction texts is to consider oppositions, contrasts or conflicts. Sometimes the conflict might be between characters, or between characters and the community in which they live or work. The community here is the school.

6 Using your annotation of the passage from Activity 4, produce either a mind map or bullet list to set out clearly the points you might include in your answer.

The following example is a list of possible points which address the three bullet points you were asked to think about when answering the question. A list such as this helps you to organise your material. Your list will be different from other students' lists, because different readers will select different details from the text. You should keep glancing back at your list and the question, as you write your full answer. This will help you to keep your ideas relevant to the question.

Impressions of Miss Brodie
- Unorthodox teacher – tells pupils to pretend they're having an English lesson – congratulates them for not answering Miss Mackay's question
- Has high standards – rolling up sleeves not 'civilised'
- Powerful effect her story of Hugh has on her pupils – all tearful
- Tells half-truths – 'We are having a history lesson'
- Sees herself as an out-of-the-ordinary teacher – can make pupils 'the crème de la crème'

Interaction with others
- With the pupils, Miss B very much the teacher
- Pupils are moved by her story-telling
- Criticises girls for scruffiness (Sandy) or for inattention (Mary)
- Third person narrator judgements on girls likely to be Miss B's – e.g. 'little pig-like eyes' (Sandy) & 'lumpy etc.' (Mary) – hints at a cruel streak?
- Clear contrast with Miss Mackay – 'Crying over a story at ten…'

Dialogue
- Sarcasm to Sandy – 'day's washing'
- Poetic treatment of Hugh's death – 'He fell like an autumn leaf'
- Miss M sees pupils as 'little girls' – unlike Miss B
- Miss B's use of colour (black/white/silver/golden) to excuse not telling truth
- Miss B's pretensions – 'crème de la crème'

7 Write a plan which sets out briefly an effective order of points for answering this question.

You could use the list of points in Activity 6, or ideas of your own, or a mixture of both.

Writing your answer

In test conditions, write out your full answer to the question, using the plan you produced in Activity 7.

Allocate your time as follows:

50 minutes writing your critical response

5 minutes checking through what you have written.

Extension

Work with a partner, reading each other's response to the question. Indicate in pencil, using the numbers below, examples of the following:

Successful features of writing
1 Points supported by textual reference
2 Analysis of words and phrases

Less successful features of writing
3 Points not supported by reference
4 Quotations used, but key words not analysed

Quick recap

The following table summarises the points you should remember when writing about Poetry and Prose unseen passages.

Key point	What it means in practice
Answer the question set.	Keep the question firmly in mind as you write. Refer regularly to the question and your plan.
Address the bullet points.	The bullets are there to help you. Make some response to each bullet point somewhere in your essay. You do not have to follow the order of the bullet points.
Focus on the writer's methods.	You need to analyse how the writer uses language, structure and their chosen form. It is not enough simply to explain the content of the printed poem or passage. You should analyse the way the material is structured within the poem or passage. Give your reader the impression that you are responding to distinctive features of Poetry or Prose – depending on which question you choose to answer.

Develop your own informed response to the passage and question.	You have to support all the points you make by providing evidence from the passage in the form of brief quotations. Simple assertions are not enough. You must justify your points.
Demonstrate skills of critical analysis.	You should not use quotations merely to illustrate the points you make. Quotations should be the starting point for precise comment on how writers use particular words to achieve their effects. Use the 'Point + Quotation + Comment' strategy to help you. You should: 1 make a point 2 support the point with a quotation 3 provide a comment on the key word(s) in the quotation.
Present your argument clearly.	The following will help you to produce a clear and well-written response: • Use a formal register • Organise your writing logically into paragraphs • Check that each sentence is clear and relevant • Write using accurate spelling and punctuation • Write legibly.

Working through a practice Unseen Paper

Tip

For the questions you have answered in this Unit, the extracts have been given line numbers, to make it easier for you to refer to the texts. In your exams, the extracts and poems on your Set Texts Paper will have line numbers, but those on your Unseen Paper will not. In order for you to become familiar with what to expect in the exam, no line numbers have been given in this practice Unseen Paper.

The following pages introduce you to the format of the Unseen Paper. In the examination, you will only answer *one* question: *either* the Poetry Unseen *or* the Prose Unseen. However, you should work through both of the questions in this practice paper. This will allow you to develop effective ways of tackling both kinds of Unseen questions. The more you practise, the more confident you will become at planning and timing your answers.

1   Read carefully the following poem which describes a man's visit to the place where his brother used to live.

How does the poet capture the speaker's feelings about his brother and the visit he made to the place where his brother used to live?

To help you answer this question, you might consider:

- what you learn of the speaker's feelings as you read the poem
- the mood created by the description of the weather
- the words the speaker addresses to his dead brother.

BROTHERS

Last night I arrived
a few minutes
before the storm,
on the lake the waves slow,
a gray froth cresting.
Again and again the computer voice said
you were disconnected,
while the wind rattled
the motel[1] sign outside my room
to gather
its nightlong arctic howl,
like an orphan moaning in sleep
for words in the ceaseless
pelting of sleet,
the night falling
to hold a truce[2] with the dark.
In the Botticellian stillness[3]
of a clear dawn I drove
by the backroads to your house,
autumn leaves like a school of yellow tails[4]
hitting the windshield
in a ceremony of bloodletting.
Your doorbell rang hollow,
I peered through the glass door,
for a moment I thought
my reflection was you
on the other side,

staring back,
holding hands to my face.
It was only the blurred hold of memory
escaping through a field of glass.
Under the juniper[5] bush
you planted when your wife died,
I found the discarded sale sign, and looked for a window
where you'd prove me wrong
signaling to say
it was all a bad joke.
As I head back, I see the new
owners, pale behind car windows
driving to your house.
You're gone who knows where,
sliced into small portions
in the aisles of dust and memory.

[1] *motel*: hotel for motorists
[2] *truce*: suspension of hostilities
[3] *Botticellian stillness*: stillness typical of a painting by Sandro Botticelli (1445–1510)
[4] *yellow tails*: white moths with yellow–tipped abdomens
[5] *juniper*: evergreen shrub

2   Read carefully the following passage, which is the opening to a novel.

How does the writer vividly portray the relationship between Mrs Rupa Mehra and her daughter?

To help you answer this question, you might consider:

*   the way the writer describes the mother and daughter
*   how the dialogue illustrates the different attitudes mother and daughter have towards marriage
*   the ways in which the writer makes the dialogue and description entertaining.

'You too will marry a boy I choose,' said Mrs Rupa Mehra firmly to her younger daughter.

Lata avoided the maternal imperative by looking around the great lamp-lit garden of Prem Nivas. The wedding-guests were gathered on the lawn. 'Hmm,' she said. This annoyed her mother further.

'I know what your hmms mean, young lady, and I can tell you I will not stand for hmms in this matter. I do know what is best. I do know what is best. I am doing it all for you. Do you think it is easy for me, trying to arrange things for all four of my children without His help?' Her nose began to redden at the thought of her husband, who would, she felt certain, be partaking of their present joy from somewhere benevolently above. Mrs Rupa Mehra believed, of course, in reincarnation[1], but at moments of exceptional sentiment, she imagined that the late Raghubir Mehra still inhabited the form in which she had known him when he was alive: the robust, cheerful form of his early forties before overwork had brought about his heart attack at the height of the Second World War. Eight years ago, eight years, thought Mrs Rupa Mehra miserably.

'Now, now, Ma, you can't cry on Savita's wedding day,' said Lata, putting her arm gently but not very concernedly around her mother's shoulder.

If He had been here, I could have worn the tissue-patola sari[2] I wore for my own wedding,' sighed Mrs Rupa Mehra. 'But it is too rich for a widow to wear.'

'Ma!' said Lata, a little exasperated at the emotional capital[3] her mother insisted on making out of every possible circumstance. 'People are looking at you. They want to congratulate you, and they'll think it very odd if they see you crying in this way.'

Several guests were indeed doing namasté[4] to Mrs Rupa Mehra and smiling at her; the cream of Brahmpur society, she was pleased to note.

'Let them see me!' said Mrs Rupa Mehra defiantly, dabbing at her eyes hastily with a handkerchief perfumed with 4711 eau-de-Cologne. 'They will only think it is because of my happiness at Savita's wedding. Everything I do is for you, and no one appreciates me. I have chosen such a good boy for Savita, and all everyone does is complain.'

Lata reflected that of the four brothers and sisters, the only one who hadn't complained of the match had been the sweet-tempered, fair-complexioned, beautiful Savita herself.

'He is a little thin, Ma,' said Lata a bit thoughtlessly. This was putting it mildly. Pran Kapoor, soon to be her brother-in-law, was lank, dark, gangly, and asthmatic.

'Thin? What is thin? Everyone is trying to become thin these days. Even I have had to fast the whole day and it is not good for my diabetes. And if Savita is not complaining, everyone should be happy with him. Arun and Varun are always complaining: why didn't they choose a boy for their sister then? Pran is a good, decent, cultured khatri[5] boy.'

There was no denying that Pran, at thirty, was a good boy, a decent boy, and belonged to the right caste[6]. And, indeed, Lata did like Pran. Oddly enough, she knew him better than her sister did – or, at least, had seen him for longer than her sister had. Lata was studying English at Brahmpur University, and Pran Kapoor was a popular lecturer there. Lata had attended his class on the Elizabethans, while Savita, the bride, had met him for only an hour, and that too in her mother's company.

'And Savita will fatten him up,' added Mrs Rupa Mehra. 'Why are you trying to annoy me when I am so happy? And Pran and Savita will be happy, you will see. They will be happy,' she continued emphatically. 'Thank you, thank you,' she now beamed at those who were coming up to greet her. 'It is so wonderful – the boy of my dreams, and such a good family. The minister Sahib has been very kind to us. And Savita is so happy. Please eat something, please eat: they have made such delicious gulabjamuns[7], but owing to my diabetes I cannot eat them even after the ceremonies. I am not even allowed gajak[8], which is so difficult to resist in winter. But please eat, please eat. I must go in to check what is happening: the time that the pandits[9] have given is coming up, and there is no sign of either bride or groom!' She looked at Lata, frowning. Her younger daughter was going to prove more difficult than her elder, she decided.

'Don't forget what I told you,' she said in an admonitory[10] voice.

[1] *reincarnation*: being born again in another body or form
[2] *sari*: garment of long cloth wrapped round the waist and passed over the shoulder and head
[3] *capital*: advantage
[4] *doing namasté*: greeting with respect
[5] *khatri*: Punjabi, from a north Indian community
[6] *caste*: social class
[7] *gulabjamuns*: popular Indian dessert
[8] *gajak*: dry sweet made from sesame seeds
[9] *pandits*: scholars skilled in Hindu religion
[10] *admonitory*: warning

Quick recap
Strategies for tackling the Unseen Paper

This flowchart shows how you can make effective use of the 1 hour 15 minutes allocated for answering the question on the Unseen Paper.

20 Minutes

Look at both questions and decide which one to answer.

⬇

Read your chosen question and highlight its key words.

⬇

Read the text, together with any glossary, keeping the question in mind.

⬇

Read the text again, highlighting and annotating key words on the question paper.

⬇

Draw a mind map *or* write a list to gather your ideas.

⬇

Write a brief paragraph plan, setting out the order of your points.

50 Minutes

Begin writing your answer by addressing the question and providing a **brief** overview of the content and structure

⬇

Develop your response to the question set, exploring language, structure and form

⬇

Use the 'Point + Quotation + Comment' strategy

⬇

Write a brief conclusion about the effect of the text as a whole in relation to the question

5 Minutes

Check what you have written.

Tip

Five minutes spent checking your work before the end of the examination allows you to:

- add points – perhaps at the end of your response, using an asterisk (*) for cross-reference
- amend points to improve the wording
- delete points – for example, where you have repeated the same point.

Unit summary

This Unit builds on the work covered in Units 3 and 4 on 'Responding to Poetry' and 'Responding to Prose'. It also builds on the skills practised in Unit 6: 'Developing effective writing skills'.

This Unit has helped you to develop a number of strategies for responding to Unseen Poetry and Prose texts. Suggested strategies include active reading, which involves highlighting key words in the question and annotating relevant detail in your chosen text. This Unit has also explained the benefits of using mind maps and lists to gather relevant material you might use in your answer.

Before writing your answer out in full, you should write a concise plan, which sets out the order of the points in your response. The Unseen Paper includes 20 minutes for these essential stages which prepare you for the main writing. The checklist in the 'Quick recap' reminds you how to arrange your timing effectively.

Once you have started your main writing, you need to focus clearly on the question rather than simply explaining the content of the text. The 'Point + Quotation + Comment' strategy will help you to support your points and to comment on the writer's use of language, structure and form. The guidance in this Unit will help you to produce an informed personal response which examiners will enjoy reading.

The next Unit will look at how you can prepare for a Set Texts paper.

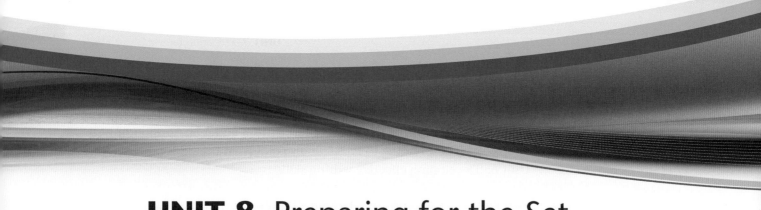

UNIT 8 Preparing for the Set Texts Papers

Objectives

In this Unit, you will:

- look in detail at the types of question set

- consider effective strategies for answering them

- use a range of strategies for active learning

- develop effective revision strategies.

What will you have to do for the Set Texts Papers?

All students of the Cambridge IGCSE Literature syllabus will sit one of the Set Texts Papers – *either* Paper 1 *or* Paper 4.

Some students may also take the other Set Texts Paper (Paper 5) if they are not doing the Coursework or Unseen options.

The following table sets out rules you must follow when sitting the Set Texts Papers.

Set Texts paper	Rules
Paper 1 2 hours 15 minutes	For this paper you must: • answer *three* questions: *one* Drama, *one* Poetry and *one* Prose • answer at least *one* passage-based question and at least *one* general essay question • You are allowed to take your texts with you into the examination. These should be clean copies, that is, without any annotation.

Set Texts paper	Rules
Paper 4 2 hours 15 minutes	For this paper you must: • answer *three* questions: *one* Drama, *one* Poetry and *one* Prose • answer at least *one* passage-based question and at least *one* general essay question You are *not* allowed to take your texts with you into the examination.
Paper 5 45 minutes	For this paper you must : • answer any *one* question on any text. You are *not* allowed to take your text with you into the examination.

How to approach set texts questions

This Unit introduces you to the different types of questions you will be asked on your set texts, and offers guidance about how to respond to them effectively.

There are *three* types of question on set texts:

• Passage-based critical questions on Drama, Poetry and Prose texts
• General critical essay questions on Drama, Poetry and Prose texts
• Empathic questions on Drama and Prose texts.

Each of these types of question requires a different approach to answering them. You have practised the skills required for all three question types in earlier Units in this Coursebook. Follow the Link features in this Unit, which refer you back to other relevant sections of the book, to recap on these skills.

We will now look at each of these question types more closely.

Passage-based questions

The first question on each set text is always a passage-based question. This question is based on a passage from your set text. In the case of Poetry questions, the 'passage' will be a single poem or an extract from a longer poem.

In the next section of this Unit you will look closely at two examples of past passage-based questions:

• The first question is based on an extract from Samuel Taylor Coleridge's poem *The Rime of the Ancient Mariner*.
• The second is based on an extract from the novel *Jane Eyre* by Charlotte Brontë.

Tip

Empathic questions focus on a particular character. Poems do not generally present characters in the way they are presented in plays or in Prose fiction, so it is not possible to set empathic questions on Poetry texts. Empathic questions are therefore set only on Drama and Prose set texts.

Link

Look back to Unit 4: 'Responding to Prose' to remind yourself about what you are asked to do in empathic responses, and for guidance on how to approach this type of question.

Link

The skills of close analysis you use for critical essays are also needed when you respond to the Poetry or Prose questions on the Unseen Paper. Remember that you will not be required to respond to unseen Drama texts. Look back to Unit 7 to remind yourself of the skills you need when responding to questions on Unseen texts.

In what ways does this illustration capture the atmosphere of Coleridge's poem?

Example passage-based question (1)

Further reading

You might like to read the complete poem *The Rime of the Ancient Mariner,* which is freely available on the internet.

Read this extract from the first part of *The Rime of the Ancient Mariner* by Samuel Taylor Coleridge, and then answer the question that follows it.

From THE RIME OF THE ANCIENT MARINER[1]

And now the STORM-BLAST came, and he
Was tyrannous[2] and strong:
He struck with his o'ertaking wings,
And chased us south along.

With sloping masts and dipping prow[3],   5
As who pursued with yell and blow
Still treads the shadow of his foe,
And forward bends his head,
The ship drove fast, loud roared the blast,
And southward aye we fled   10

And now there came both mist and snow,
And it grew wondrous cold:
And ice, mast-high, came floating by,
As green as emerald[4].

And through the drifts the snowy clifts   15
Did send a dismal shccn[5]:
Nor shapes of men nor beasts we ken[6] –
The ice was all between.

The ice was here, the ice was there,
The ice was all around: 20
It cracked and growled, and roared and howled,
Like noises in a swound!

At length did cross an Albatross[7],
Thorough the fog it came;
As it had been a Christian soul,   25
We hailed it in God's name.

It ate the food it ne'er had eat,
And round and round it flew.
The ice did split with a thunder-fit;
The helmsman[8] steered us through!   30

And a good south wind sprung up behind;
The Albatross did follow,
And every day, for food or play,
Came to the mariners' hollo!

In mist or cloud, on mast or shroud,   35
It perched for vespers nine[9];
Whiles all the night, through fog-smoke white,
Glimmered the white Moon-shine.

'God save thee, ancient Mariner!
From the fiends, that plague thee thus! –   40
Why look'st thou so?' – With my cross-bow
I shot the ALBATROSS.

1 **mariner** person who navigates a ship

2 **tyrannous** oppressive (unjustly cruel)

3 **prow** front part of ship

4 **emerald** a gemstone of great value

5 **sheen** reflection of light

6 **ken** saw

7 **Albatross** large sea bird

8 **helmsman** person who steers the ship

9 **vespers nine** early evening

Link

For exam questions on set text passages, the meanings of difficult words are not given. You should already be very familiar with the text, and have found these out for yourself. For the passages in this Unit, from *The Rime of the Ancient Mariner* and *Jane Eyre*, unfamiliar words have been explained to help readers who may not be familiar with the texts.

You will see that in Unit 7: 'Preparing for the Unseen Paper', unfamiliar words have been explained in the practice exam questions. This is to help you as a reader of a poem or extract you have not seen before.

Now read the following question carefully, before you go on to the next section:

How does Coleridge create a mysterious atmosphere in these lines?

Analysing the passage-based question (1)

This question is based on an extract from Coleridge's long poem *The Rime of the Ancient Mariner*. You only have to focus on the lines in the extract, as the wording 'in these lines' makes clear.

There are two clues in the question that tell you to focus on the way the writer uses language, structure and form:

- The question begins with 'How …?'
- The mention of the poet's name.

Tackling the passage-based question (1)

The skills required to answer this question are similar to those tested in the Unseen Poetry question. The difference here is that you would already be very familiar with the passage, as it is from one of the set texts. The time allowed for answering the question is therefore less than for the Unseen Paper.

For each set text question you should spend 45 minutes on your answer. The first five minutes should be spent reading the passage carefully, and noting the words and phrases you will quote and comment on in your answer.

Tip

Remember that your comments on the effects of particular words should be developed in some detail in order to achieve higher marks.

Tip

In poetry it is always useful to look carefully at the way in which the poet uses individual stanzas within the overall structure of the poem.

From the examinations in 2012 onwards, passages will be printed on all Set Texts papers. This means you can highlight the words and phrases you intend to quote.

The following are the key requirements for a successful answer to this passage-based question:

- Keep the essay relevant to the main thrust of the question – how Coleridge creates a mysterious atmosphere
- Pay attention to the detail of the passage
- Use many short quotations from the passage
- Comment on the effects achieved by Coleridge's use of language and poetic form
- Comment on the development of stanzas within the extract
- Develop an informed personal response.

Example passage-based question (2)

Read the following extract from Charlotte Brontë's *Jane Eyre*, and then answer the question that follows it.

There was no possibility of taking a walk that day. We had been wandering, indeed, in the leafless shrubbery an hour in the morning; but since dinner (Mrs Reed, when there was no company, dined early) the cold winter wind had brought with it clouds so sombre, and a rain so penetrating, that further outdoor exercise was now out of the question.   5

I was glad of it; I never liked long walks, especially on chilly afternoons; dreadful to me was the coming home in the raw twilight, with nipped[1] fingers and toes, and a heart saddened by the chidings[2] of Bessie, the nurse, and humbled by the   10
consciousness of my physical inferiority to Eliza, John, and Georgiana Reed.

The said Eliza, John, and Georgiana were now clustered round their mamma in the drawing-room: she lay reclined on a sofa by the fireside, and with her darlings about her (for the time   15
neither quarrelling nor crying) looked perfectly happy. Me, she had dispensed[3] from joining the group, saying, 'She regretted to be under the necessity of keeping me at a distance; but that until she heard from Bessie, and could discover by her own observation that I was endeavouring in good earnest[4] to acquire   20
a more sociable and child-like disposition, a more attractive and sprightly manner – something lighter, franker, more natural, as it were – she really must exclude me from privileges intended only for contented, happy little children.'

'What does Bessie say I have done?' I asked.   25

1 **nipped** cold
2 **chidings** scoldings
3 **dispensed** excused
4 **in good earnest** seriously

5 **cavillers** those who raise trivial objections

6 **moreen** heavy, woollen

Charlotte Brontë (above) had two sisters, Emily and Anne, who were also famous writers.

'Jane, I don't like cavillers[5] or questioners; besides, there is something truly forbidding in a child taking up her elders in that manner. Be seated somewhere; and until you can speak pleasantly, remain silent.'

A small breakfast-room adjoined the drawing-room, I slipped in there. It contained a book-case; I soon possessed myself of a volume, taking care that it should be one stored with pictures. I mounted into the window-seat: gathering up my feet, I sat cross-legged like a Turk; and, having drawn the red moreen[6] curtain nearly close, I was shrined in double retirement.

Folds of scarlet drapery shut in my view to the right hand; to the left were the clear panes in glass, protecting, but not separating me from the drear November day. At intervals, while turning over the leaves in my book, I studied the aspect of that winter afternoon. Afar, it offered a pale blank of mist and cloud; near, a scene of wet lawn and storm-beat shrub, with ceaseless rain sweeping away wildly before a long and lamentable blast.

30

35

40

Now read the following question carefully before you go on to the next section:

In what ways do you think Brontë makes this an effective opening to the novel?

Analysing the passage-based question (2)

The focus here is slightly different from that in the question on Coleridge. That question required analysis of just the passage itself.

For the question on Brontë, you should in fact spend *most* of your time analysing the detail in the passage. The extract is referred to as 'this' in the question. However, in order to comment on how effective the passage is as an opening to the novel as a whole, you would need to make some reference to what happens later in the book.

As in the Coleridge question, there are two big hints that make it clear you must focus on the way Brontë uses language, structure and form:

- The question begins with 'In what ways ...?'
- The mention of the novelist's name.

Tackling the passage-based question (2)

As with the Coleridge question, five out of the 45 minutes for the Brontë question should be spent reading the passage carefully, and noting the words and phrases you will use in your answer.

Tip

Students who get lower marks in passage-based questions have generally failed to engage fully with the detail in the extract. The key to success in addressing the question is to:

• make many brief references to the passage

• provide detailed comment about the effects created by the writer's use of form, structure and language.

Link

Unit 6: 'Developing effective writing skills' sets out an approach to critical writing (see pages 137–40). Here is a brief re-cap of the main points:

• Know your text in detail

• Understand what the question is asking for

• Keep your answer relevant to the question

• Select your points

• Use textual detail to support them

• Analyse the writer's use of language, structure and form.

Tip

Students taking Open book examinations should certainly use brief quotations from their texts. However, they must not be tempted to copy out long sections of the text. Focusing on short quotations leads to clearer and more precise analysis.

The following are the key requirements for a successful answer to this passage-based question:

• Keep the essay relevant to the main thrust of the question – the ways Brontë makes the passage an effective opening to the novel

• Pay attention to the detail of this Prose passage

• Use many short quotations from the passage

• Comment on the effects achieved by Brontë's use of language

• Comment on the effects of using first person narrative viewpoint

• Comment on the development of the material within this crucial opening passage

• Develop an informed personal response.

 # General critical essays

General essay questions test the same skills of close analysis as passage-based questions and Unseen questions. The major difference is that passages are not provided for general essay questions. Instead, you have to select the material from the text to answer the question that has been set.

Students taking Paper 1 are allowed to take a clean copy of their set texts into the Open book examination, whereas students of Papers 4 and 5 are not allowed access to texts in these Closed book examinations. Examiners are often impressed by just how many quotations students are able to remember in their answers for the Closed book Papers 4 and 5. Remember that short quotations (one word or a short phrase) are better than long ones. There is no need to memorise large chunks of the text. Examiners cannot give credit for long quotations that have simply been copied out. In fact, shorter quotations are likely to lead to more precise analytical comment. If you cannot remember a particular quotation, do not panic. Refer instead to a key detail from the text to support your point.

Analysing the general essay question

The following table lists some typical past general essay questions, together with advice about how to tackle them. You are not expected to recognise the writers or characters in the questions below, although they may be familiar to you. Instead, focus on the wording of the questions and read the guidance on how to approach each one.

Tip

Questions often include words which are designed to make you think about the quality of the writing. In the examples given here there are words such as *vivid, compelling, memorable* and *dramatically*. Other words which may be used in questions include the following:

- tense
- moving
- important
- significant
- striking
- amusing
- ironic
- powerful

These are words which you should consider carefully, since they direct your attention to how writers present their subject-matter: for example, in the way they present characters or themes and ideas.

Question	How to tackle the question
How does Lee make Tom Robinson's conviction so unjust?	The word 'How?' encourages you to look carefully at the ways Harper Lee uses language, structure and form. This is not a simple invitation to write about the trial scene or give a character sketch of Tom Robinson.
In what ways does Williams make Stanley such a dramatically compelling character?	The 'In what ways?' encourages you to consider carefully Tennessee Williams' use of language, structure and form. The use of the word 'dramatically' further reminds you that the text is a play. You are being invited to write about what makes Stanley such a powerful presence ('dramatically compelling') on the stage. You could usefully consider how Stanley appears to the audience at different stages in the play. A straightforward character sketch or re-telling of Stanley's important scenes in the play will not be enough to answer this question.
*Explore the ways in which poets use imagery to memorable effect in **two** of the following poems:* Caged Bird (*by Maya Angelou*) Rising Five (*by Norman Nicholson*) Before the Sun (*by Charles Mungoshi*)	The command word 'Explore' is another way of encouraging you to examine in detail writers' use of imagery. The question makes it clear that you must write about two poems from the list of three. You cannot score high marks if you only write about one poem, and you waste your time if you write about all three poems listed. Paraphrases, or explanations of content, will receive only low or average marks. Close analysis of words and their effects is required to achieve higher marks.
To what extent does Hansberry encourage you to sympathise with Walter?	The clear focus on the writer requires you to look closely at the dramatic methods Lorraine Hansberry uses in order to depict the character of Walter. The opening words of the question ('To what extent?') might lead to answers which find Walter a character who is very sympathetic, not sympathetic at all, or both, in different parts of the play. An effective approach would be to sift the evidence carefully before reaching an informed personal judgement.

Question	How to tackle the question
'A wicked and violent criminal' 'A victim of injustice' *Which of these views do you think more accurately describes Dickens' presentation of Magwitch?*	This question invites you to consider two prompts which are possible views of the character of Magwitch in Charles Dickens' novel *Great Expectations*. The phrase 'Dickens' presentation' reminds you to consider his use of language, structure and form in bringing the character vividly to life. As with the previous question, an effective approach would be to consider both views before reaching an informed judgment of your own.
Explore the ways in which the author vividly portrays a lonely woman in a dreadful relationship in **either** *Samphire (by Patrick O'Brian)* **or** *A Stranger from Lagos (by Cyprian Ekwensi). Refer to the detail of your chosen story in your answer.*	The word 'Explore' tells you to examine in detail the ways in which the writer of your chosen short story uses language, structure and the short story form. The question makes it clear that you must write on one of the stories. You would receive no extra credit for writing about both stories.

Tackling the general essay question

For general essay questions, as for other types of question on the Set Texts Papers, you should allow 45 minutes, and you should aim to spend up to five minutes of this time planning your answer. There are two steps you should follow in your planning:

- Highlight the key words of the question on the question paper
- Create a brief plan in your answer booklet.

The following are the key requirements for a successful critical essay:

- Keep the essay relevant to the question
- Select persuasive evidence from the text to support your answer
- Comment on the effects created by the key words and phrases in your quotations
- Comment on the writer's use of structure
- Comment on the writer's use of form
- Develop an informed personal response.

Tip

A plan is for your benefit. Use abbreviations which you understand. Do not become so involved in your plan that it becomes longer than your answer!

Unit 6: 'Developing
effective writing skills'
sets out an approach to
writing empathic responses
(see pages 142–49).

Empathic questions

Empathic questions are set on all Drama and Prose texts. They encourage
a more creative engagement with the ways in which writers write.
All empathic questions ask you to take on the role of a particular character.
You need to write in a voice that is entirely appropriate for the character.

Here is a brief re-cap of the main points to remember when writing a
response to an empathic Literature question:

- Know your text in detail
- Analyse the question carefully and understand what it is asking
- Focus on the character's thoughts:
  - at the moment given in the question
  - about other characters
  - about events which are relevant to them
- Adopt a suitable voice for the character
- Adopt a suitable voice for the moment specified.

Analysing the empathic question

Here are three examples of empathic questions:

You should avoid writing
thoughts that a character
would not have at the
moment specified in the
question. Knowing the
sequence of events is part
of your appreciation of the
structure of the text.

1 You are Lady Macbeth, just after the banquet has come to such a
   disastrous end. You are now alone. Write your thoughts.
2 You are Benjamin at the end of the book [*Animal Farm*], just after you
   have read to Clover the sole remaining commandment. Write your
   thoughts.
3 You are Blanche towards the beginning of the play [*A Streetcar Named
   Desire*]. You are on the streetcar on the way to your sister's apartment.
   Write your thoughts.

Many empathic questions give a particular moment during the course of
the play, novel or short story. Sometimes the chosen moment may be the
end of the text.

Note that each question ends with the instruction 'Write your thoughts'.

Tackling the empathic question

As with the general essay question, you need to spend five of your
45 minutes thinking and planning before you start to write your answer.

You need to consider carefully the following:

You should avoid the
following, which are
common weaknesses
in students' answers to
empathic questions:

- Being vague about the
  particular moment in the
  question
- Straying from the world of
  the text
- Failing to capture a
  recognisable voice for the
  character
- Failing to convey
  development of the
  character's thoughts.

- The moment given in the question
- Events that happen from the character's perspective
- The thoughts the character might have at that moment in the text.

Your plan could once again take the form of bullet points or a mind map.

The following are the key requirements for a successful empathic answer:

- Keep the moment clear in your mind
- Root your answer in the detail of the text
- Write in a voice that readers will recognise as appropriate for the character
- Develop an informed personal response.

 Link

Remember – the skills tested in passage-based questions and general essay questions are largely the same. There is, however, one significant difference:

- In passage-based questions, you are given the passage
- In general essay questions, you select suitable material from relevant parts of the text.

Quick recap
How to write successful answers to set text questions

Critical responses to passage-based and general essay questions

Look at the mind map below to remind you of the points to remember for writing a successful critical response to a passage-based or general essay question.

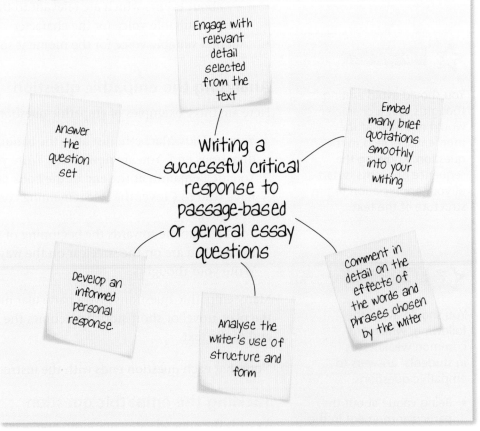

Empathic responses

Look at the mind map below to remind you of the points to remember for writing a successful response to an empathic question.

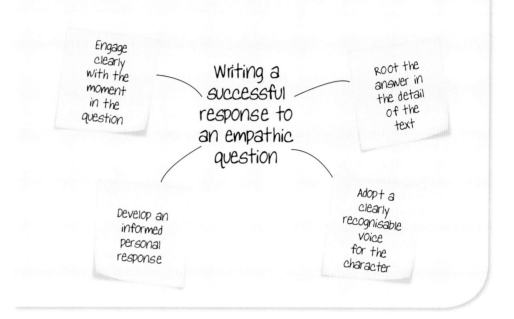

⊙ Be an active learner!

Perhaps the most useful way to start this section is to say what active learning is *not*!

Here are some examples of very inefficient ways of learning:

- Reading a set book from cover to cover without making any notes
- Reading or writing with the television on or with music playing
- Studying without removing distractions (such as your cellphone and social networking)
- Writing essays without doing a plan first
- Plagiarising.

Students who are passive learners will not do much more than skim the surface of a text and will rely on the opinions of their teacher or from study guides. Passive learning may lead to the following:

- A limited knowledge of your set texts, without much detail
- Insufficient focus on writers' choices about language and structure
- Relying on others' ideas rather than your own informed personal response.

Here are some suggested strategies for active studying. These can help you to take greater responsibility for your own learning, and become an active learner!

Active learning strategies

Read with a pen in your hand

Be prepared to write notes. Remember your first impressions, and see whether they change as you re-read the text. Make a point of looking up the meaning of difficult or unfamiliar words. If your teacher allows you to, annotate your edition of the text (or perhaps photocopies of important pages). But remember, that you cannot take an annotated text into the examination room.

Initiate your own research

Read about your set texts and authors in the library or by using the internet. Ask yourself the following question: Does what you read confirm or challenge your own views?

Use the internet wisely. After searching for a particular topic, read a few of the recommended web pages. Try to work out which sites are the most useful and reliable. Remember the following:

- Do not copy others' ideas. Read or listen to what others have to say, and work out whether you agree with them or not. In this way, you can work towards an *informed* personal judgement.
- Do not copy chunks of material from books or the internet. This is cheating.

Listen to texts as well as reading them

Read poems aloud. Poets make deliberate choices about sounds in order to convey their feelings and ideas.

Listen also to the words spoken by characters in plays and novels or short stories. Read some of their words aloud in order to capture the way they speak. This is good practice for empathic questions as it allows you to get beneath the skin of characters.

Audio texts have become very popular. Where they exist, good audio versions of your set texts can enrich your study. They can help you to appreciate how particular words or lines might be spoken.

Watch texts as well as read them

You might be very fortunate and have the opportunity to see the play you are studying performed in the theatre or at your school. You can of course visualise how a particular scene might be performed as you read it in class.

Many plays and novels have been adapted into films. You should certainly take an interest in how film makers have interpreted texts you are studying. Films can be obtained in DVD format or downloaded from the internet, and clips of key moments can usually be found.

Tip

After your initial study of poems and major speeches by characters in plays, try the following: practise reading the poems and speeches aloud, getting the right emphasis for every word. Aim for a polished performance. You could do this with a friend, and you could even record your performance!

Baz Luhrmann's 1996 film of Shakespeare's *Romeo and Juliet* took creative liberties with the text. The feud between the Capulets and Montagues involved gunfights against the backdrop of petrol stations.

Watching a film in its entirety, or just clips from a film, can enhance your reading of the text. It should not, however, replace your reading. There is a very good reason for this: film scripts may not be faithful to the original texts. You should note any differences between the book and film versions. When writing essays, always make sure you write about the text of the novel or play you have studied closely during the course, and not a film version of it.

Developing effective revision strategies for your set texts

The final section of this Unit will suggest some effective strategies you might adopt for revising your Drama, Poetry and Prose texts.

The aims of revision are as follows:

* To develop an increasingly detailed grasp of the text's content and structure
* To grow more confident in exploring the writer's use of language and form
* To build up a wide range of reference you can use to support points in critical and (for Prose and Drama texts) empathic writing.

Drama

A play, when performed in the theatre, might last for two to three hours. After your initial study of the play in class, you should aim to re-read the play two or three times before the examination. Because you know the play already, you should be able to **skim read** the text. In this way, you can focus on the important scenes and speeches.

As you read, consider carefully how the words might be spoken. Visualise how particular scenes might be performed on stage. You might also have an audio or video version to supplement (though not replace) your learning of the text.

Your files may contain an assortment of your own notes, essays, handouts from your teacher or printouts containing material from the internet. You need to organise these various items of information carefully in your files. During your revision, you may need to retrieve a specific item – for example, an essay about a particular character. If your filing is effective, you should be able to find the item easily.

After your initial study of the play in class, you should follow this up with the focused strategies suggested on the following pages.

Key term

Skim read means to 'read rapidly'. After your close study of a text, you should be able to skim read it, which will allow you to concentrate on key parts of the text.

Tip

Keep your files tidy and organised. Your 'file' may well be a physical thing that you carry home and to your classroom or it may be a virtual file that you can access by computer at home and at school. You may have both a physical file and a virtual one.

Link

You may have already used the 'Quotations and Comments' strategy when working through earlier Units. You may have used it as a way of recording information when planning a response to questions on Poetry, Prose and Drama texts.

Here it is suggested that you use the same strategy for revision purposes when preparing for your Set Texts exam.

Make notes on characterisation for your set text

No Cambridge IGCSE Literature question will ask you to give a simple character sketch. Questions on characters will focus on the ways in which the writer *presents* the character, for example:

Explore the ways in which Shakespeare makes Macbeth's brutality as king so terrifying.

Two effective ways of assembling useful revision material for this question are:

- Mind maps
- 'Quotation and Comments' tables.

a A mind map such as this could provide a useful starting-point for more detailed revision:

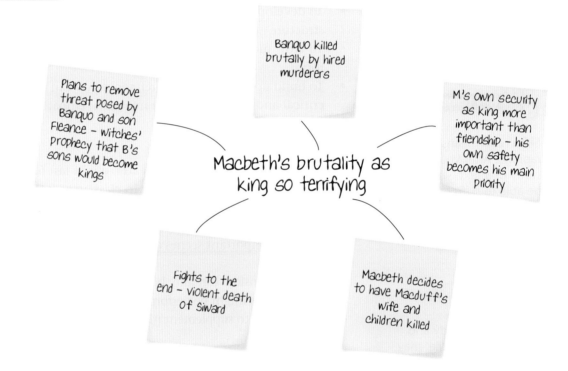

b   Here are two entries from a 'Quotation and Comment' table that help
    to focus on the detail of the language:

Act & scene	Quotation	Comment
Act 3, Scene 4	First murderer describes the 'twenty trenchèd gashes' in Banquo as 'The least a death to nature'.	The violence of Banquo's death is a direct consequence of Macbeth's paying the murderers to kill him. Just one of the twenty gashes would have been sufficient to kill him, which shows the level of brutality.
Act 4, Scene 1	After witnessing the apparitions, Macbeth vows to: '... give to th' edge o' th' sword / His wife, his babes ...'	In order to remove the threat posed by Macduff, Macbeth pledges to kill Lady Macduff and her children. The phrase 'give to th' edge o' th' sword' provides a graphic indication of their imminent deaths. It also shows Macbeth's complete lack of morality.

Make up your own passage-based questions

a   Select *four* key extracts from your set play text. Each extract should be
    about two pages long.

Using the play *Macbeth* as an example, you might select extracts which
show how Shakespeare:

•   presents a key character, such as Banquo
•   presents the relationship between two characters, such as Macbeth and
    Lady Macbeth
•   develops an important theme, such as the tyranny of Macbeth's
    kingship
•   establishes the setting or mood, for example, the scene in which
    the witches summon the monstrous apparitions.

As part of your close study, you should analyse these extracts carefully.
This will help you to practise the skills needed for passage-based questions.

b   For *two* of your chosen extracts, focus exclusively on analysing the
    extract. You could use questions such as the following:

Explore the ways in which the writer makes this passage so amusing / horrifying / powerful / dramatic [or choose another adjective which is suitable for the passage you have chosen].

c For the other *two* extracts, try this question:

How does the writer make this such a dramatic and significant moment in the play?

The second question has a slightly different focus from the first. The main focus is still on analysing how the extract is *dramatic*, but there is an additional focus: here you need also to make some comment on how the moment is *significant* within the play as a whole. The second question encourages you to consider the position of the extract within the structure of the whole play.

d Practise the necessary skills of quoting and commenting by highlighting and annotating copies of your chosen extracts.
e Work in pairs. Ask your partner to read and annotate your response to one of the passage-based questions. Then discuss each other's efforts.

Make up your own empathic questions

a Choose *two* characters from your play.

For each character select a key moment, which is *not* the end of the play.

Then construct your own empathic questions.

Use the following wording as a template:

You are _____, just after_____.
Write your thoughts.

b For both your empathic questions, practise the necessary skills by writing the thoughts the character would have at the chosen moment.
c In pairs, try out one of your questions as a hot-seating activity.

Poetry

Here are some suggestions for the best ways of revising the poems in your chosen Poetry collection. For each poem:

- Have a clean copy
- Assemble all of your notes and any extended writing you have done on the poem
- Read the poem carefully
- Using all the information you have, annotate the clean copy of the poem.

Tip

Remember: no empathic questions are set on poems.

In the example below, taken from Coleridge's *The Rime of the Ancient Mariner*, you can see the following annotation:

- Notes on content (in blue)
- Notes on language, structure and form (in green)
- Useful quotations (highlighted in yellow).

> Sailors surrounded by ice. Terrifying noises made by the ice.

> Personification of the ice – suggests a frightening animal

> Simile describing noises as heard by someone fainting – 'swound' an archaic word close to 'swoon' (faint)

> Repetition of 'ice' making use of ballad form

> Examples of onomatopoeia evoking strange and frightening noises – horrifying to the sailors

The ice was here, the ice was there,
The ice was all around:
It cracked and growled, and roared and howled,
Like noises in a swound!

The notes you produce at this stage will help you to give an informed personal response to the way the poets convey their subject matter. Your notes will be *informed* by the following:

- Earlier research you may have undertaken
- Your readings in class
- Discussions you have had in class.

Extension

For this exercise you could work with a partner or in small groups.
Each of you should select *one* poem. Then:

- Practise reading it, paying close attention to the sounds of words and pace of lines
- Make an audio recording of your reading.

Because by now you know the poems in such detail, it can be a good time to record the poems being read aloud. Listening to the recordings can provide an excellent form of revision.

Prose

A long novel can take a good deal of time to read – much longer than a Drama text. It might not be possible to read every page in class. In practice it is usually only possible in class to study very closely a number of pages from the book.

After your initial study of your Prose text, you should aim to re-read it two or three times before the examination. After the first reading, you should be able to skim read it, pausing to concentrate and spend more time on studying the important sections. These will be pages where:

- characters are introduced or developed
- there is a twist or turn in the plot

- important themes are developed
- setting and mood are clearly established.

After your initial study of the Prose text in class, you should follow this up with these focused strategies:

Make notes on characterisation for your set text

As with your Drama set text, arrange your characterisation notes by using the following:

- Mind maps
- 'Quotation and Comment' tables.

Make up your own passage-based questions

a   Select *four* key extracts from the novel you are studying. If you are studying the collection of ten short stories from the *Stories of Ourselves* anthology, choose *one* key extract from *four* of the stories. Each extract should be one to two pages in length.

Using Harper Lee's novel *To Kill a Mockingbird* as an example, you might select extracts which show how the writer:

- presents a key character, such as Calpurnia
- presents the relationship between two characters, such as Atticus and Scout
- develops an important theme, such as the poisonous effects of racial prejudice
- establishes the setting or mood, for example, in the courtroom scene where Tom Robinson is tried
- uses narrative viewpoint, for example, in Scout's account of her first day at school.

As part of your close study, you should analyse these extracts carefully. This will help you to practise the skills needed for passage-based questions.

b   For *two* of your chosen extracts, focus exclusively on analysing the extract. You could use questions such as this one:

Explore the ways in which the writer makes this passage so comic / disturbing / ironic / dramatic [or choose another adjective which is suitable for your chosen passage].

c   For the other *two* extracts, try this question:

How does the writer make this such a memorable and significant moment in the story?

This question has a slightly different focus from the last one. The main focus is still on analysing how the extract is *memorable*, but there is an additional focus: you need to make some comment on how the moment is *significant* within the novel or short story as a whole. This question encourages you to consider the position of the extract within the structure of the overall text.

d Practise the necessary skills of quoting and commenting by making use of highlighting and annotation on copies of the extracts.

e Work in pairs. Ask your partner to read and annotate one of your passage-based questions. Then discuss each other's efforts.

Make up your own empathic questions

a Choose *two* characters from your set text. If you are studying the short stories collection, choose *one* character from *two* different stories.

For each character select a key moment.

Then construct your own empathic questions.

Use the following wording as a template:

You are _____, just after_____.
Write your thoughts.

b For both questions, practise the necessary skills by writing the thoughts the character would have at the chosen moment. The skills being tested here are the same as for empathic questions on characters in play texts.

c In pairs, try out one of your questions as a hot-seating activity.

Tip

Remember that Drama texts are intended for performance on a stage, whereas Prose fiction texts are intended for personal reading. This will affect how you visualise what is happening in the play, novel or short story.

Link

For a reminder of how 'hot-seating' activities work, look back to the Extension Activity on page 104 of Unit 5: 'Responding to Drama'.

Quick recap
Strategies for revising set texts

Revision strategies for Drama and Prose texts
- Make notes on characterisation and main themes
- Practise skills of close reading on selected extracts from the text
- Devise your own passage-based questions
- Devise your own empathic questions

Revision strategies for poems
- Annotate a copy of each poem for content
- Annotate a copy of each poem for the writer's use of language, structure and form
- Read the poem aloud as if for performance
- If you have time, make a recording of the poem to assist your revision

Tip

The form of a poem needs to be considered differently from the form of a play or story. Look again at pages 36–37 in Unit 3: 'Responding to Poetry'.

Unit summary

This Unit has built on the work you have already done in the earlier Units on responding to Poetry, Prose and Drama.

In this Unit, you will have developed a number of strategies to help you prepare for a Set Texts paper. These strategies include active reading, annotating texts, writing a plan, and seeing or listening to texts. You can also make your own recordings of poems and key extracts from texts as part of your own revision. You will also find it useful to devise your own practice questions.

Revision is more effective if you have organised your files carefully.

The guidance given in this Unit will help you to produce your own informed personal responses to the set texts you are studying.

UNIT 9 Preparing for the Coursework portfolio

Objectives
In this Unit, you will:

- find out what is required for your Coursework portfolio

- learn how to approach reading and researching your Coursework texts

- learn about effective strategies for planning, writing and presenting your written assignments.

Link

If you are doing the Coursework option, you will also be preparing for Paper 1, the Open book Set Texts Paper.

Link

Go back and read through Unit 6: 'Developing effective writing skills'. This will remind you of the different requirements for writing both critical essays and empathic responses to texts.

About your Coursework

This Unit provides you with all the information you need to produce your Coursework portfolio. You should think of your Coursework as an integral part of your Literature course rather than something separate or added on as an extra item. Coursework will help you to develop reading and writing skills that are also necessary for the Set Texts examination.

Coursework allows you and your teacher a good deal of flexibility, as the school chooses the texts you read and the assignments you do. You are encouraged to do independent research as well as discussing in lessons your ideas about your chosen text and topic. Coursework requires you to think carefully about the writing process – from note-making through planning your work to the presentation of the final version of your essay. The skills you develop in your Coursework will also be useful in other subjects and as preparation for study after IGCSE.

Key term

Assignment is the term used for a piece of written work you have to do as part of your study.

Portfolio refers to your two completed Coursework assignments.

Assignment title refers to the question or topic you have been set for your work.

What will you need to do for your Coursework portfolio?

The main requirement is for you to produce *two* written **assignments** for your Coursework **portfolio**.

Key points to remember:

- Your assignments can be on texts from any of the three main literary forms: Drama, Poetry or Prose.
- Your assignments can be critical essays or empathic responses.
- You should follow the guidance given by your teacher about the length of your assignments.

The following sections provide more detail about the requirements for your assignments.

Choosing your assignment titles

Your teacher will make sure that each **assignment title** is worded in such a way that you can meet all the assessment objectives of the course.

Here are some examples of general essay titles that lack a clear focus and would *not*, therefore, allow students to show the skills necessary for close analysis of literature:

1 *Macbeth*
2 '*Dulce et Decorum Est* and *Disabled'*
3 'What happens in *Lord of the Flies?'*
4 'The character of Blanche in *A Streetcar Named Desire'*

Examples 1 and 2 are simply titles of texts: a play by Shakespeare and poems by Wilfred Owen. The assignment title needs to make clear the particular aspects of the texts you are going to write about.

Example 3 asks for a simple re-telling of the plot of *Lord of the Flies*. This assignment title has an inadequate focus since it does not invite an analysis of the novelist William Golding's use of language, structure or form.

Whilst Example 4 does indicate a specific character, it does not provide a specific focus for study of that character. Writing about the 'character of Blanche' in general is likely to lead to a simple list of the character's traits; it would be difficult to award marks to such a response.

Compare these with the following examples, which provide a more specific and focused topic for students to investigate. These assignment titles

Tip

Make sure that you put your assignment title in full at the top of the front page of your assignment. This is essential information for those teachers and examiners who read your assignment.

highlight the importance of the writer. The wording of these titles points students in the right direction. They enable students to write about the ways in which writers use form, structure and language to convey their meanings.

1 Explore the ways in which Shakespeare presents the murder of Duncan and Banquo in *Macbeth*.
2 How does Wilfred Owen memorably convey the horror of war in *Dulce et Decorum Est* and *Disabled*?
3 How does William Golding make Jack and Roger such terrifying characters in *Lord of the Flies*?
4 In what ways does Tennessee Williams make Blanche such a dramatically compelling character in *A Streetcar Named Desire?*

Choosing your texts

- Each assignment should be on a different text.
- One of your assignments may be on a text studied for your Set Texts examination paper.
- Your two texts may be from the same literary form: for example, they may both be plays.
- An assignment on Poetry must include reference to two poems. Similarly, an assignment on short stories must include reference to two stories. The poems or stories can be discussed separately; there is no need to compare.

How to present your portfolio

Assignments may be typed or handwritten. You should check your work carefully for errors.

You should include any references to secondary source material (such as study guides in print or online) at the end of the assignment. Remember to indicate clearly if you are quoting directly from any secondary source.

You should give the details of a book using a standard convention for bibliographies, for example:

McCarthy, S (1999) *Poems of Seamus Heaney*, Hodder & Stoughton.

In this example, the information is presented in the following order:

Surname and initial of first name → Date of publication in brackets → Title in italics (or underlined if you are writing your assignment by hand) → Name of publisher.

In the case of online texts, you should give the precise web page and in brackets write the date you accessed it, for example:

http://www.Poetryarchive.org/Poetryarchive/singlePoet.do?poetId= 1392 (20 July 2011)

If you are using a word processor, it is easy to copy the URL address and paste it straight into your document.

Tip

Generally speaking, a Poetry assignment must refer to *two* poems and a short story assignment must refer to *two* stories. However, there are exceptions where the poems or stories are lengthy: for example, Coleridge's poem *The Rime of the Ancient Mariner* or Dickens' story *A Christmas Carol*.

Using your preparation time effectively

Getting to grips with the detail

Know your texts

The first stage is to work towards a clear and detailed understanding of your text.

You will find it useful to have your own copies of poems and stories or key passages of novels and plays. You can use these copies for the following purposes:

- For highlighting or underlining useful textual references
- For annotating key words with your own impressions about characters and ideas, and to highlight details in the text.

Be selective

Remember that for the Coursework assignment you do not need to study the complete text closely. You should concentrate on those parts of the text which are relevant to the topic in your assignment title. You cannot say everything there is to be said. You must, therefore, be selective. In order to respond effectively to the assignment title you have chosen, you should focus on a number of key ideas. It is better to develop a few points in detail than try to cover too many points which lack development. If there are too many points, they can become rather disconnected, and lack focus. Fewer, more developed points can give a clearer focus to your writing.

Develop your own ideas

Your teacher is likely to provide opportunities for you to discuss your ideas with other students during lessons. Such discussions allow you to develop your own informed personal response. Your own views will be confirmed or challenged by what others have to say.

Private study

You should also take advantage of time allocated for private research and study. You may, for example, wish to consult study guides to help you clarify details of the plot or characters. It is fine to do this, so long as you remember not to copy material from study guides or indeed any other material you refer to.

Make notes

You should also spend a significant amount of time re-reading relevant parts of your text carefully and making notes on them. Notes at this stage

Plagiarism is copying down other people's words and passing them off as your own. It is a kind of theft – stealing the words or intellectual property of others. You must never be tempted to do this. If you do this and are found out, you could be disqualified from the examination. Schools and examination boards use sophisticated software to detect plagiarism.

There are many accessible study guides in book form or online. They can help you clarify certain aspects of the texts you are studying. You should keep a note of any study guides or other sources that you refer to. Any reference you make to this material has to be listed at the end of your assignment (as shown on page 193).

Link

In Unit 7: 'Preparing for the Unseen Paper' a mind map was used to arrange relevant material for a question on Liz Lochhead's poem *The Choosing* (page 154). Here, a table is used to gather appropriate material. When sorting relevant material for your assignment, you should use a method which works best for you.

Tip

It is a good idea at the note-making stage to keep a record of relevant page numbers so that you can easily locate references for your essay when you write or word process the first draft.

You should not, however, refer to page numbers in your essays. This is because the edition you are using might be different from the edition your reader uses.

Tip

In the Set Texts examination papers, empathic questions are set only on Drama and Prose texts. This is because plays and novels (or stories) include characters whose voices can be readily captured in empathic writing.

might usefully be presented in bulleted or numbered lists, mind maps or perhaps tables.

The following table provides an example of how you might present your notes for this assignment on *Lord of the Flies*:

How does William Golding make Jack and Roger such terrifying characters in Lord of the Flies?

Page No.	Character	Textual evidence	Comment on how Golding makes such terrifying characters
41	Jack	'He snatched his knife out of the sheath and slammed it into a tree trunk.'	Golding's use of aggressive words such as 'snatched' and 'slammed' suggest how easily Jack might become violent.
78	Roger	When Roger throws stones in the direction, he aims to miss: 'Yet there was a space round Henry, perhaps six yards in diameter, into which he dare not throw.'	At this stage of the novel, Roger is still restrained by the values of home and school. Later in the novel, he has no such restraint, and there are disastrous consequences for Piggy.

For critical essay assignments, make notes on the following:

- Relevant characters and themes in plays, novels and short stories
- Key ideas or feelings expressed in poems
- How the writer uses form
- How the text is structured
- Effects created by using particular words and phrases (including imagery and sound).

You learned in earlier Units how important it is to consider *how* writers write as well as *what* they write. You need to appreciate technique as well as content. Make sure at this stage that you have selected references from the text to support each of your points.

For empathic assignments, make notes on the following:

- Key aspects of the chosen character
- Their relationship with other characters
- Ways in which the character is linked to key themes
- Language and tone of voice typically used by the character.

Link

The guidance given here on sorting your material and putting your ideas in a logical order links with the guidance given in Unit 6: 'Developing effective writing skills'. Coursework allows you to practise and sharpen these key skills which will be equally important in the Set Texts Paper.

Tip

Work out, by looking back at another piece of work you have written, how long a 1000-word piece of work is in typescript or in your own handwriting. Keep this in mind during both the preparation and writing stages. An IGCSE Literature Coursework essay of 1000 words is long enough to be able to gain a top grade; overly long work can lose focus and become rambling.

For empathic assignments, the notes you make will help you to produce a clearly recognisable voice for your character. Everything your character says must be rooted in a close reading of the text.

Selecting your information

You need to arrange from your notes the points and quotations or references you intend to use to answer the assignment title. At this stage, you are likely to spend some time considering whether to include or delete various points.

If you have done the previous stage successfully, you will find you have too much information. So you will need to decide which points and references you should include, and which to cut out.

The following mind map sets out a possible plan for the assignment on *Lord of the Flies* on page 195, making clear the various areas that you might consider. Remember that this is just one possible plan. Other readers might respond to the same question using a different plan. There is no right answer, just different ways of approaching the question. The mind map below is for the character of Roger. A similar plan could be used for the character of Jack.

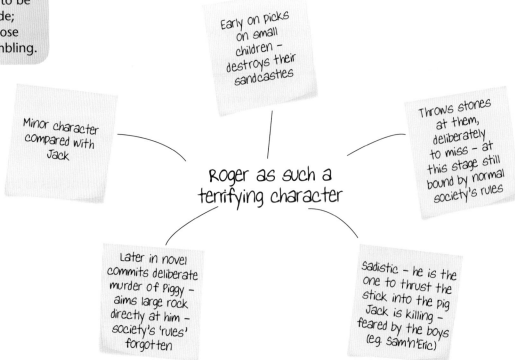

You might find it helpful to look back at Unit 6: 'Developing effective writing skills' for more guidance on how to plan your writing and put your information in a logical order.

Putting your ideas into a logical order

This stage of your work is about putting the points you wish to make into the most logical order. A flowchart might be a useful way of expressing your thoughts at this stage. You may need to revise your flowchart more than once as you consider the most effective way of structuring your material. You will refer regularly to your flowchart as you write your first draft. Remember that you may need to make further adjustments to your work during the actual writing, and there is nothing wrong with doing that. After all, you are working to produce your highest standard of work.

Putting your material in a logical order is important whether you are writing a critical essay or an empathic response. In a critical essay there should be a clear and logical line of argument, with each point connected to the previous and next points. In an empathic response you will need to consider structure in much the same ways writers do, in order to create a suitable impact for your reader.

Jack's first appearance in the novel – leading the exhausted choir

How Jack develops into terrifying character as the novel progresses – his obsession with hunting – his cruel treatment of Piggy

How Roger is presented early in the novel – still guided by rules of civilisation – throwing stones to miss

The extreme cruelty of Roger as the novel develops

The importance of these two characters to the novel – what they represent about aspects of human nature

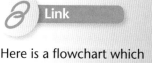

Here is a flowchart which provides one possible plan for the question. This provides a clear structure for the *Lord of the Flies* essay.

⦿ Writing your response

Writing your first draft

Writing an assignment of this length can seem quite daunting. But the preparation you have done so far should give you confidence to go ahead and tackle this. You are likely to write your first draft in stages rather than all at once. As you write, make sure that you are free from distraction. This is particularly important if you are working at home. Do not allow yourself to be distracted by music, television, text messages or emails.

Make sure that you have the following near to hand:

- Copies of your texts (including copies of key pages)
- Your notes and flowchart
- A good dictionary (which may be in print or online).

With coursework assignments, you should take the opportunity to plan thoroughly. You have to be selective about the detail you include in your writing. This practice at planning is a skill that will be useful when you come to sit your exam paper. For exam questions there are two main differences:

- You will not be able to plan in such detail
- You will need to be even more selective.

In the first paragraph of your assignment, you should engage directly with the key words of the assignment title. There is no need for any background information about the writer or period in which they were writing. You should not worry if you do not get your introduction absolutely right at this stage. You can return to it later.

As you write your first draft, it is important to keep the following questions in mind.

For critical essays
- Is each point you make supported by relevant reference to the text?
- Is each quotation as concise as it can be? Have you quoted only those words you need to illustrate your point?
- Are you analysing the effects of key words on the reader (or 'audience' if the text is a play)?
- Do you move from one point to another in a logical sequence?
- Is each sentence clearly focused on the task?
- Are you using paragraphs effectively to help structure your argument effectively?

For empathic responses
- Is each sentence something your chosen character might say?
- Is each sentence rooted in the world of the text? It is not appropriate in an empathic response to introduce new events, characters or settings.
- Are you using words and phrases that are typical of your character in the text?
- Do you move from one point to another in a logical sequence?
- Are you using paragraphs to help structure your response effectively?

Tip

Remember you do not need to quote from the text in an empathic response. If you do, it is likely to affect the flow of your own writing, which should capture the character's thoughts.

Amending your flowchart

As you write your first draft, you may need to amend your flowchart. This is a perfectly acceptable and sensible thing to. Your mind has had more time to reflect on the task and how best to respond to it.

Re-drafting your first attempt

At this stage, when checking your work it is best to work on a copy of your first draft using different coloured pens. This means that you can annotate it in a number of ways as part of your re-drafting. You might make use of the following:

- Wavy underlining to indicate unclear expression
- A straight line through words to be deleted
- Asterisks to indicate where words, sentences or paragraphs are to be added
- Arrows to indicate words or sentences you wish to move.

There are a number of points that you need to address at the re-drafting stage. These are summarised in the following tables.

For all assignments

Points to remember	What to do about it
Is your assignment within the word limit?	You may find you have to cut material out at this stage. You must make the necessary deletions, and not your teacher. This is good practice for any extended writing tasks you are likely to do in a range of subjects both at this level and after IGCSE.
Is every sentence focused on the title?	If not, amend or delete the sentence. You will not receive credit for points that are not relevant to the title.
Are your paragraphs and connectives used effectively?	You need to pay close attention to: - how your paragraphs are structured - the connectives you use to link the ideas in your sentences and paragraphs.
Are your punctuation and spelling accurate?	Check the spelling and punctuation in your work. Accurate use of English helps the reader to focus on the content of your answer without being distracted by errors.

The points listed here are also useful to remember when checking your essay in an exam. Remember that you will have less time to make any revisions in the exam than for your Coursework assignment!

Look back at Unit 6: 'Developing effective writing skills' (page 128) for further guidance on checking your work effectively.

An **assertion** is when someone confidently states a view without providing evidence to support it. In Literature, it is important for you to go beyond assertion. You must support your view by reference to relevant detail in the text.

For general essay assignments

Points to remember	Guidance
Are your points supported by reference to the text?	Check that the points you have made are always supported by relevant textual references. If you do not provide textual evidence, you will find you are simply writing **assertions**. This leads to your writing being descriptive rather than analytical.
Do you analyse structure and language in your essay?	You need to demonstrate a clear appreciation of *how* writers communicate their meanings. Make sure you explore the effects created by writers' use of: • a particular structure • specific words and phrases.
Have you commented on how the writer uses their chosen form?	You should explore how writers use Drama, Poetry or Prose to communicate their meanings.
Are quotations smoothly integrated into your sentences?	Brief quotations should be inserted smoothly into your sentences without interrupting the flow of your writing.
Is your essay in suitably formal English?	Avoid informal English such as contractions (e.g. don't, hasn't) and the use of slang and clichés. You should not, for example, refer to Jack in *Lord of the Flies* as a 'psycho', or Macbeth's 'game plan' in getting rid of Banquo!

For empathic assignments

Points to remember	Guidance
Is there any aspect of the 'voice' that strikes a jarring note?	If there are words or phrases that do not really suit the character, cut them out.
Are the language and tone appropriate for the character's voice?	You may include the occasional word or phrase used by the character in the text. This will make the voice recognisable. Your writing should persuade your reader that they are listening to a voice that is appropriate for the character.
Is the organisation of your material clear and logical?	Your reader should be convinced by the flow of the character's thoughts. Your writing should persuade them that they are listening to a voice that is appropriate

Points to remember	Guidance
	for the character at the moment mentioned in the question. For example, Macbeth would not necessarily think in a logical or organised way after just having murdered Duncan.
Is your response rooted clearly in the world of the text?	You should not go beyond the world of the text. So do not introduce new events, characters or settings. Everything you write should be related to the world of the text.

Presenting your final version

At this stage your aim is to produce a polished version of your work to hand to your teacher for marking. As you write or type, there is still the opportunity to make improvements. But all the hard re-drafting work will have been done during the previous stage. You need, of course, to do a final read through of your work to check the accuracy of spelling, punctuation and grammar.

Some students choose to write their essays by hand, which is fine, but your work must be written clearly and legibly, preferably in black or dark blue ink.

Remember that all assignments should include the following:

- Your name and candidate number
- The full wording of the task (and not an abbreviation or approximation of it)
- Margins that are sufficiently wide for teachers to add their comments
- Page numbers
- A word count at the end of the essay
- (Where appropriate) a list of references at the end, to include any secondary source material you have used in your work.

If you are using a word-processor for your work, you will find the following checklist useful:

- Use a clear and readable black font
- Have left and right margins wide enough for your teacher's comments
- Leave a space between block paragraphs
- Use the spell check and grammar check functions carefully, making sure that any replacements still give the right words and meanings
- Use italics for titles of texts.

Tip

Avoid the use of fancy fonts, for example, fonts that look like old-fashioned writing for assignments on Shakespeare. Remember that it is important to do all you can to communicate clearly with your reader. New Times Roman (12-point) and Arial (11-point) are excellent fonts for this purpose:

'New Times Roman'
'Arial'

Quick recap

This flowchart will help to remind you of the key stages in producing a Coursework assignment.

Read closely those parts of the text
relevant to the task

List useful references and make brief comments
on the writer's techniques

Write a plan which puts the material in a logical order

Write the first draft

Re-draft, checking that your argument is clear and
that your English is accurate

Present your final version to your teacher

Unit summary

This Unit has set out the requirements of the Coursework portfolio. You have been guided through the process of producing a Coursework assignment. For you, this process starts with the close reading of those parts of the text relevant to the task. It ends with the production of the polished version of your assignment which you hand to your teacher.

This Unit explained the importance of making notes and listing relevant references for use in your assignments. Mind maps, lists and tables provide effective ways of gathering relevant material. The Unit also stressed the need to work out the most effective way to structure a clear line of argument in critical writing or a clear progression of thoughts in empathic writing. Only then can the writing of the first draft begin.

The active reading and writing skills you will develop in your Coursework also provide excellent preparation for the Set Texts Paper. In Coursework you have more time to focus on and develop these essential skills, which will also be useful in other subjects and in your future studies.

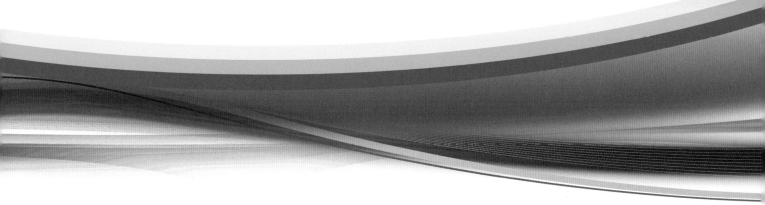

Glossary of key terms

Each term is followed by the page number where it first appears in this book.

Alliteration The repetition of consonant sounds in words that are close together. **30**

Analysis The close exploration of the words writers use and the effects these words create for the reader, of Poetry and Prose texts, and for the audience of Drama texts. **14**

Annotate Make notes providing brief explanations or comments. **5**

Archaic words Words which are no longer in use, or whose meaning has changed over time. **15**

Assertion When someone confidently states a view. In critical essays, evidence from the text must be used to support that view. **200**

Assignment The term used for a piece of written work you do if you are taking the Coursework option. **192**

Assignment title The question or topic set for your work, if you are taking the Coursework option. **192**

Assonance The repetition of vowel sounds in words that are placed close together. **33**

Back story What happens in a character's life before the action of a play or novel starts. **107**

Characterisation The ways in which writers present their characters. **58**

Conflict Struggles or disagreements between characters that can often be found at the heart of plays. These help to create tension, making a scene particularly dramatic, and engaging the attention of the audience. **102**

Critical responses Answers that consider evidence in the text and weigh up different arguments. **55**

Dialogue The words spoken by the characters, usually in Prose or Drama. **59**

Direct speech The words actually spoken by characters in Prose texts. These are usually indicated by the use of speech marks around the words the characters speak. For example, *'It is a clump of samphire, Molly,' he said.* **62**

Dramatists Writers of plays. Another commonly used term is 'playwright'. **95**

Empathic responses Answers that show understanding and sympathy for characters and try to imagine what it would be like to be a particular character in a play, novel or short story. The word 'empathy' means the ability to understand and share the feelings of others. **55**

Enjambment Occurs where lines of poetry run on without punctuation and without a break in the meaning. **41**

First person narrator An actual character in the novel. All the events of the novel are told from this character's viewpoint. We see events and other characters through their eyes. **78**

Free verse Verse which has irregular lines and lacks a regular metre. **39**

Hyperbole The use of exaggeration for a deliberate effect. **45**

Imagery You can often picture in your head the images created by the words a writer uses in a text. Some types of imagery are not so obvious, and writers use them to communicate their ideas more vividly; for example, see **simile**, **metaphor** and **personification**. **28**

Interpretation How directors and actors offer a particular 'reading' of how characters' lines might be spoken or actions performed on the stage. **96**

Metaphor Rather than using words such as 'like' to compare things, a metaphor says that one thing *is* actually another. **29**
Mood Created by writers through their use of description and dialogue. Another word for mood is 'atmosphere'. **74**

Narrative Narrative techniques are the ways in which a story is told. **66**
Narrator The person who tells the story in a novel or short story. What happens is communicated through their words. **78**

Onomatopoeia A word which sounds like the thing it describes. **30**
Overview A general statement about the content of a text or extract. **22**

Pace The speed at which a particular line of poetry is read. It can also refer to the speed at which one line follows another. **106**
Performance Bringing to life the words on the page for an audience in a theatre. **96**
Personification When something inanimate is given human (or animal) characteristics. **29**
Plot The storyline of a novel, short story, play or narrative poem. **66**
Portfolio Your two completed assignments, if you are taking the Coursework option. **192**
Props Short for 'properties', these are items used in performances of plays. **96**

Quatrain A group of four lines, usually rhyming. **36**

Register The level of formality in writing. **139**
Rhetorical question A question used for effect, requiring no answer. **118**
Rhyme The use of similar sounds for words or endings of words: for example 'trees' and 'breeze', and 'hills' and 'daffodils'. **33**

Rhyming couplet Two consecutive lines of poetry that rhyme with each other. **36**
Rhythm A regular pattern of long and short sounds, words or lines in poetry. **14**

Senses These enable us to experience the world around us. Writers often use words which appeal to our senses of sight, hearing, touch, smell and taste. They do this to make their writing more vivid for the reader. **74**
Setting Where the action of a text takes place. It is where the characters' thoughts, words and actions are situated. There may be more than one setting, and a particular setting may change as the text progresses. **71**
Short story Shorter than a novel, a short story generally concentrates on a single event and has a small number of main characters. **57**
Simile One thing compared to another. It is easy to spot similes, as they signal comparison by using the words 'like', 'as' or 'as if'. **29**
Skim read To read rapidly. **183**
Sonnet A poem of 14 lines, each having ten syllables. **36**
Stage directions These provide information to directors, actors and others involved in bringing a playscript to life on the stage. **101**
Stanza A group of lines within a poem. **14**
Strategies Approaches you use when studying texts effectively. **16**
Stream of consciousness A particular technique Prose writers can use to convey a person's mind as it moves from one thought to another. The effect is like being able to listen to a character's thoughts in real time. **78**

Tense The form of a verb, which shows the time when an action happened. For example, 'She stopped' is past tense, so the action of stopping occurred in the past; 'She stops' is the present tense, where the action is taking place now. **71**
Text When used in this Coursebook, this refers to a poem, short story, novel or play. When studying English Language, you might work on different types of texts, such as letters and newspaper articles. **1**

Theme The word used to explain the deeper meanings of a text. Common themes in Literature are childhood, love, conflict, war, the passage of time, death, ambition, deception, and the list goes on. **75**

Third person narrator Often referred to as an omniscient (or all-knowing) narrator. This type of narrator is able to comment on everything that all characters say, think and do. **80**

Tone This is conveyed in a text by the writer's deliberate choice of words. The tone can change as a text develops. **41**

Turning-point A twist that signals a change in direction or a change in tone in a text. **23**

Acknowledgments

The authors and publishers acknowledge the following sources of copyright material and are grateful for the permissions granted. While every effort has been made, it has not always been possible to identify the sources of all the material used, or to trace all copyright holders. If any omissions are brought to our notice, we will be happy to include the appropriate acknowledgments on reprinting.

With thanks to the following for permission to reproduce copyright text material:

p. 17: 'Afternoons' by Philip Larkin from *The Whitsun Weddings*, published by Faber and Faber Ltd, 1964, reprinted by permission;

p. 21: 'Plenty' by Isobel Dixon, from *A Fold in the Map*, published by Salt Publishing Ltd, 2007, © Isobel Dixon;

p. 27: 'Blackberry-Picking' by Seamus Heaney from *Death of a Naturalist*, published by Faber and Faber Ltd, 1966, reprinted by permission;

p. 40: 'Telephone Conversation' by Wole Soyinka, copyright © 1962, 1990 by Wole Soyinka, reprinted by permission by Melanie Jackson Agency LLC;

p. 48: 'Row' by Carol Ann Duffy from *Rapture*, published by Pan Macmillan, London © Carol Ann Duffy, 2005;

p. 49: 'Wind' by Ted Hughes from *Remains of Elmet*, published by Faber and Faber Limited, 1979, reprinted by permission;

p. 56: from 'The Hitch-hiker', from *The Wonderful Story of Henry Sugar and Six More* by Roald Dahl, copyright 1945, 1947, 1952, 1977 by Roald Dahl Nominee Limited; copyright renewed 2005 by Felicity Dahl, Chantal Sophia Dahl, Theo Dahl, Ophelia Dahl, and Lucy Faircloth Dahl, used by permission of Alfred A. Knopf, an imprint of Random House Children's Books, a division of Random House, Inc. and published by Jonathan Cape Ltd and Penguin Books Ltd, used by permission of David Higham Associates Ltd;

p. 59: Extract from 'Samphire' by Patrick O'Brian, from *Collected Short Stories* © Patrick O'Brian 1953, reproduced by permission of Sheil Land Associates Ltd and HarperCollins Publishers Ltd;

p. 64: from *A Stranger from Lagos* by Cyprian Ekwensi, licensed by David Bolt Associates;

p. 69: from *The Siege* by Helen Dunmore, by permission of AP Watt Ltd on behalf of Helen Dunmore;

p. 72: from *The Lemon Orchard* by Alex la Guma, © 1962 Estate of Alex la Guma, reprinted by permission of the author and the Sayle Literary Agency;

p. 76: from 'Studies in the Park' by Anita Desai from *Games at Twilight and Other Stories*, copyright (c) 1978 Anita Desai, reproduced by permission of the author c/o Rogers, Coleridge & White Ltd, 20 Powis Mews, London W11 1JN;

p. 85: *The Pieces of Silver* by Karl Sealy, by permission of Beryl (wife), Roger and Trevor, family of the late Karl H Sealy;

p. 98: from *The Glass Menagerie* by Tennessee Williams, copyright © 1945, renewed 1973 by The University of The South, reprinted by permission of Georges Borchardt Inc for the Estate of Tennessee Williams;

p. 104: from *Death of a Salesman* by Arthur Miller, copyright © 1949, renewed 1977 by Arthur Miller, reproduced by permission of Wylie Agency and Viking Penguin, a division of Penguin Group (USA) Inc;

p. 109: from *A Taste of Honey* by Shelagh Delaney, © 1959 Shelagh Delaney and Methuen Drama, an imprint of Bloomsbury Publishing Ltd, reprinted by kind permission of the author and the Sayle Literary Agency;

p. 123: from *A Streetcar Named Desire* by Tennessee Williams, copyright © 1947 The University of the South, reprinted by permission of Georges Borchardt Inc for the Estate of Tennessee Williams, and New Directions Publishing Corp., all rights reserved;

p. 141: 'Farmhand' by James K. Baxter;

p. 154: 'The Choosing' by Liz Lochhead; from *Dreaming Frankenstein and Collected Poems 1967-1984*, published by Polygon, 2003;

p. 158: from *The Prime of Miss Jean Brodie* by Muriel Spark, published by Penguin, reproduced with permission;

p. 164: 'Brothers' by G.S. Sharat Chandra;

p. 166 from *A Suitable Boy* by Vikram Seth, copyright © Vikram Seth, 1993, published by The Orion Publishing Group, London, by permission of David Godwin Associates.

Thanks to the following for permission to reproduce copyright photographs:

p. 16: Mainpicture/Alamy; p. 24: Hervé Champollion/akg-images; p. 27: David Hosking/FLPA; p. 31: Ashley Cooper/Alamy; p. 34: Dove Cottage, The Wordsworth Trust; p. 36: © The British Library Board C.21.c.44 or G.11181; p. 38: Library of Congress/Public Domain; p. 40: Elena Elisseeva/Shutterstock; p. 50: © The British Library Board FG3017-1; p. 60: Bob Gibbons/FLPA; p. 66: Vinicius Valle/photographersdirect.com; p. 70: Ria Novosti; p. 77: Omimages/Werli Francois/photographersdirect.com; p. 80: Mary Evans Picture Library/Alamy; p. 83: American Playhouse/RGA; p. 98: Nigel Norrington/ArenaPAL (Apollo Theatre, London, 2007, director Rupert Gould); pp. 104 (Birmingham Repertory Theatre, 2000, director Di Trevis), 114 (Birmingham Repertory Theatre, 1995, director Bill Alexander), 126(*l & r*) (Strand Theatre, London, 1995, director David Thacker; Young Vic Theatre Company/Lyric Hammersmith, 2005, director David Lan): Donald Cooper/Photostage.co.uk; p.120: The Art Archive/Victoria and Albert Museum, London/Eileen Tweedy; p. 109: © Moviestore Collection Ltd/Alamy; p. 121(*l & r*): AF Archive/Alamy; p. 123: Warner Bros/RGA; p. 130: Getty Images; p. 133: © The British Library/Heritage-Images/Imagestate; p. 160: 20th Century Fox/Everett/Rex Features; p. 172: Mary Evans Picture Library; p. 175: Ann Ronan Picture Library/HIP/Topfoto; p. 182: Pictorial Press Ltd/Alamy.